UNINTENDED CONSEQUENCES

THE IMPACT OF MIGRATION LAW AND POLICY

UNINTENDED CONSEQUENCES

THE IMPACT OF MIGRATION LAW AND POLICY

Edited by Marianne Dickie,
Dorota Gozdecka and Sudrishti Reich

Australian
National
University

PRESS

ANU PRESS

Published by ANU Press
The Australian National University
Acton ACT 2601, Australia
Email: anupress@anu.edu.au
This title is also available online at press.anu.edu.au

National Library of Australia Cataloguing-in-Publication entry

Title: Unintended consequences : the impact of migration law and
                  policy / editors: Marianne Dickie,
                  Sudrishti Reich, Dorota Gozdecka.

ISBN: 9781925022445 (paperback) 9781925022452 (ebook)

Subjects: Emigration and immigration.
                  Emigration and immigration law.
                  Social history--21st century.
                  World politics--21st century.

Other Creators/Contributors:
                  Dickie, Marianne, editor.
                  Reich, Sudrishti, editor.
                  Gozdecka, Dorota Anna, editor.

Dewey Number: 304.809

Cover design and layout by ANU Press.

Contents

Introduction

Marianne Dickie

The law of unintended consequences is a common adage widely understood by laypersons and academics alike. For academics, particularly sociologists and economists, it provides a useful tool to explain complexities resulting from government policy and law. For the less reverential, it can be laid alongside Murphy's law as a self-evident outcome that can provide a perfect lens through which to view and analyse complex reactions to and impacts of change.

The 1936 groundbreaking analysis of this concept by sociologist Robert Merton in 'Unanticipated Consequences of Purposive Social Action'[1] began a long history of deliberate exploration of the unanticipated, unexpected, and unintended consequences of purposeful action that arise from a complex range of factors, and impact in a variety of ways upon society and the individual.

Merton provided us with a definition for an unanticipated consequence and, importantly, established that the definition does not rest solely upon outcomes that impact negatively. Unanticipated consequences can be simultaneously positive and negative; the desirability or otherwise of the effect is often in the eye of the beholder. Merton's analysis identified five reasons for unexpected consequences, the first being that a simple mistake made through lack of knowledge of a specific situation can, in turn, prevent the accurate prediction of an outcome. The second is the assumption that repeating something that was done in the past will produce the same result in the future. Thirdly, Merton considered that unintended consequences can result

---

1   Robert K Merton, 'The Unanticipated Consequences of Purposive Social Action' (1936) 1(6) *American Sociological Review* 894.

from an action based on the need for an immediate solution, considered so urgent that the decision to ignore outcomes is deliberate. Fourthly, actions arising from what Merton terms 'basic values' in one area of life or society may be so pervasive that they prevent consideration of impacts on other areas of life or individuals. Finally, Merton coined the term 'self-fulfilling prophecy' to describe 'a false definition of the situation evoking a new behaviour which makes the originally false conception come true'.[2]

For those working within the field of migration as practitioners, academics, politicians, and commentators, the vista seems crowded with unintended consequences. In Australia, migration law is a dynamic, highly politicised, cutting-edge area of practice. As members of a migration nation, Australians feel an innate right to regularly participate in and instigate policy and legal changes to migration through social media and commentary. This often leads to outcomes that have the opposite outcome of the original intention, prompting government to implement corrections that, in turn, have unexpected impacts. At other times, legislation is implemented to achieve a specific aim that deliberately ignores consequences, intended or otherwise. For these amongst other reasons, the law of unintended consequences provides a useful analytical tool for examining migration law.

Australia's history as a geographically defined nation with control over its borders has pushed successive governments to place migration law and policy at the forefront of the political agenda. As a consequence, migration law and policy has become divided into two distinct mechanisms: one for regulating the selection of migrants, and one for regulating the behaviour of migrants once they are selected. This has become increasingly evident as Australia's migration program has moved from an emphasis on permanent skilled and family migration to an emphasis on temporary migration. The shift has included a reliance on two-stage processes that lead to permanent migration, increasing the number of individuals holding temporary visas, such as those on student visas, work visas, and holiday visas. In recent times, temporary status has also been applied through various mechanisms to asylum seekers and refugees.

---

2   Ibid.

This book arose from an inaugural conference on migration law and policy at ANU College of Law, held in October 2013.[3] The conference brought together academics and practitioners from a diverse range of disciplines and practice. The book is based on a selection of the papers and presentations given during that conference. Each chapter highlights one or more of Merton's five reasons behind unintended consequences. Each explores the unexpected, unwanted, and sometimes tragic outcomes of migration law and policy, identifying ambiguities, uncertainties, and omissions affecting both temporary and permanent migrants.

Together the chapters present a range of perspectives, providing a sense of urgency that focuses on the immediate political consequences of changes to the Australian migration program, and exposing the daily reality for individuals and society as a whole. Merton's analysis allows us to view each of these chapters in a different light, examining how these outcomes may have come into being.

Each paper chosen for the book addresses issues that are fundamental to contemporary debates about the global nature of migration in the Australian context. As a whole, they create a single text discussing the problem of the controversial nature of migration law and value judgements made by law-makers when considering potential migrant cohorts. Such judgements inevitably impact on individuals who become entangled in the migration process.

The book focuses on the control mechanisms evolving in migration law and policy, and the barriers these create for those who arrive or are already living in Australia. From language tests, to long processing times affecting the arrival of close relatives, to the obvious challenges raised by the immigration detention regime, the landscape is riddled with contradictions and uncertainty. Each author elaborates on these contradictions and explicates the uncertainties arising from the contemporary design of migration law and policy.

---

3   Please note that as these papers were written in 2013, many of the links for the reference articles were valid at the time of writing. Those no longer able to be accessed due to departmental changeover or other circumstances have been identified as 'discontinued'.

Our authors explore situations where legislation or policy purposefully drafted to remedy one problem has created new and unforeseen problems. They consider circumstances where the tension between politics and legal frameworks may have resulted in outcomes that work to undermine the law, principles of justice, or are in direct conflict with the intent of the legislation put into place by parliament.

In this way, they identify gaps and contradictions — which suggest fear and prejudice, rather than tolerance and fairness — that continue to lie at the foundation of contemporary migration law and policy. These prejudicial fears are based on the assumption that floodgates of migration will be opened to all who want to move to more privileged states.[4] Law based on fear results in the creation of an asymmetrical ethical and legal relationship between the 'we' (the receiving population) and the 'other' (the incoming migrants).[5]

By exploring the uncertainties and deep state of tension inherent in contemporary measures employed in the management of incoming migration flows, authors expose the ever increasing cracks emerging between migration law, international law, and internationally recognised human rights standards. In doing so, they challenge the contemporary regime and ask how far the cracks, tensions, and uncertainties can grow before they negatively impact on the rule of law. Their perspectives will provide the reader with a passionate, technical, and practical analysis of complex policy and legislation.

Some of the authors in the book consider how law and policy changes designed to restrict the intake of migrants can impact heavily on those who are already residing in Australia. Born out of a need to address a range of perceived political problems, these changes have resulted in an uncertain migration outcome for a range of temporary residents, and have resulted in migrants searching for new and innovative ways to remain in Australia.

---

4   Penelope Mathew, 'The Shifting Boundaries and Content of Protection: The internal protection alternative revisited' in Satvinder S Juss (ed), *The Ashgate Research Companion to Migration Law, Theory and Policy* (Ashgate, 2013) 189.
5   Costas Douzinas and Ronnie Warrington, 'A Well-Founded Fear of Justice: Law and Ethics in Postmodernity' (1991) 2(2) *Law and Critique* 115, 133.

Chapter 1, 'Pathways to Illegality, or What Became of the International Students', by Sanmati Verma, considers the effects of temporary migration, exposing how legislation and policy made in what Merton terms 'the imperious immediacy of interest'[6] can result in outcomes that benefit one sector whilst impacting negatively on others. Verma maps the growth, collapse, and reformation of the international education industry, noting in particular the surge in the vocational education and training sector, fuelled by migration policies linking Australian education with a permanent resident outcome. She traces the current rise of a permanent illegal class of residents made up of former students created from this deliberate use of migration visas to encourage overseas students, and explores what has become of this group, and its impact on the economic and political landscape. Verma's analysis allows us to see the cascading effect and ongoing consequences of changes designed to meet one goal.

In Chapter 2, Sudrishti Reich continues an examination of the plight of former international students in 'Great Expectations and the Twilight Zone: The Human Consequences of the Linking of Australia's International Student and Skilled Migration Programs and the Dismantling of that Scheme'. Reich's chapter expands on the theme of a lost generation of foreign youth. These are the self-named 'G5rs', former students demanding a resolution to their plight caused by the reversal of policy designed to counter the 'success' and unintended outcomes of the scheme that created a direct pathway from student status to permanent residence. She amplifies these students' voices, echoing their pleas from the social media and blogs that detail their despair at the years they have wasted waiting for resolution of their ambiguous visa status. Through a careful analysis of legislation, policy, speeches, media statements and social media, Reich exposes the ludicrous nature of the legislative changes that have occurred as a result of 'reactive over-compensation'.

Shanthi Robertson continues this analysis of a policy designed to achieve one outcome in Chapter 3, 'Intertwined Mobilities of Education, Tourism and Labour: The Consequences of 417 and 485 Visas in Australia'. Through a study of the life and work experiences

---

6   Merton, above fn 1.

of people on temporary work visas in Australia, Robertson exposes how the government's intent to promote temporary residence as the only goal in migration conflicts with the goals of the temporary migrant. She demonstrates how temporary residents are travelling through capillary pathways to reach their ultimate destination, creating new social and economic enclaves that silently impact on the broader community.

The silence is given voice by Peter Mares's chapter 'Unintended Consequences of Temporary Migration to Australia'. Mares discusses students, temporary workers, and the tenuous position of New Zealand migrants in Australia. Through the stories of individuals caught up in these legislative and policy paradigms, he highlights how legislation based on political will inevitably produce results that impact on legal, administrative, and institutional structures outside of and independent of the intended policy area. Mares argues that a continued reliance on a temporary program, which denies any pathway to citizenship for long-term residents, will ultimately result in an increasing range of negative social and economic outcomes. By exposing the gaps and weaknesses of the temporary migration program, he raises important moral questions that need to be confronted by Australia as a society.

Nowhere is the unintended consequence of legislation made clearer than in the poignant case of *Tahiri v Minister for Immigration and Citizenship*. Surely this must be a consequence born of error. It is clearly a piece of legislation that has resulted in an outcome that could not be predicted. Joanne Kinslor explores this in 'Reconsidering What Constitutes Objective Decision-making About Children Crossing International Borders'. Kinslor's analysis of *Tahiri* reveals how a legal provision in the migration legislation — Public Interest Criterion 4015 — which was designed to protect children in accordance with international law, has inadvertently resulted in a domestic law that can discriminate against women and leave children living in danger. She demonstrates that the crucial regulation, which is purposefully intended to give effect to Australia's obligations under the Hague Convention in matters related to child custody, applies across all visa applications. The unintended results are that the domestic law of countries not signatory to the convention is included in all visa decisions affecting child custody. Kinslor calls for a legal acknowledgement of the importance of evaluative judgements in decision-making, and highlights the need for a timely review of laws that impact negatively on those they are intended to protect.

Benjamin Powell in Chapter 6 argues that limiting migration makes no economic sense. 'A Brief Case for Open Borders in Australia' sets the scene for academics and practitioners to think outside of the box when considering unanticipated outcomes. Through the eyes of an economist, Powell challenges the myths that migrants will take jobs, drive down wages, and create a drain on the budget. He provides examples of solutions that could challenge Australia's current approaches to work, wages, and social security — solutions that may, in turn, lead to more unintended consequences.

From yet another point of view, Desmond Manderson's 'Not Drowning, Waving: Images, History, and the Representation of Asylum Seekers' takes the reader through a harrowing journey of perspectives, highlighting the role of images in determining the way we view and react to specific laws and policies that should call into question our basic humanity. In this thought-provoking chapter, Manderson forces us to contemplate our complicity and ultimate responsibility for policy deliberately designed to harm, and demonstrates the need to embed in decision-making the requirement not just for evidence, but the consideration of outcomes from as many viewpoints as possible.

Peeling back the law to expose the true impact of policy and legislation on society and individuals is the only way we can truly understand the reality of Australia's immigration system. It has been too easy to dismiss international students, asylum seekers, and temporary residents as people who want to scam a system or jump a queue. Our authors have explored the reality of immigrants' lives, exposed the law, and examined its consequences. They have challenged us to truly see what is happening, and to acknowledge the humanity of those affected. In doing so, the concept of a law of unintended consequences has provided an excellent lens through which to examine and challenge the sometimes absurd or harmful consequences of migration law and policy.

Bibliography

Beck, Ulrich, *Risk Society: Towards a New Modernity* (Mark Ritter trans, Sage, 1992)

Douzinas, Costas and Ronnie Warrington, 'A Well-Founded Fear of Justice: Law and Ethics in Postmodernity' (1991) 2(2) *Law and Critique* 115

Mathew, Penelope, 'The Shifting Boundaries and Content of Protection: The Internal Protection Alternative Revisited' in Satvinder S Juss (ed.), *The Ashgate Research Companion to Migration Law, Theory and Policy* (Ashgate, 2013) 189

Merton, Robert K, 'The Unanticipated Consequences of Purposive Social Action' (1936) 1(6) *American Sociological Review* 894

1

Pathways to Illegality, or What Became of the International Students

Sanmati Verma

Introduction

This chapter maps the growth, collapse, and reformation of what is termed the 'international education economy' — representing an array of interests spanning states and institutions (most Australian universities, Technical and Further Education (TAFE) and Vocational Education and Training (VET) providers, education and migration advice industries) — and worth at its height around $18.6 billion to the Australian economy.[1] More specifically, it seeks to document what has become of the particular representative group of international students who came into focus through mass self-organised protests in 2009 and 2010 — predominantly Indian and Chinese students working

---

1   Those who followed economic reporting on international education over the past five years cannot have failed to notice the significant variance in estimates regarding the precise value of this key 'export industry' to the Australian economy. This figure derives from reporting of Australian Education International (AEI), a branch of the Department of Education, Science and Training. See Australian Education International, 'Research Snapshot: Export Income to Australia from Education Services 2010–2011' (November 2011).

in Australia's service economy (cabs, convenience stores, contract cleaning, labour hire, sex work, etc.) and enrolled in vocational courses offered by private education providers.

Mapping the significant shifts in the Australian economy and migration policy that brought this cohort into existence, this chapter attempts to follow what has become of these several thousand temporary migrants, as migration laws and regulations were changed from 2009 onwards specifically to thwart their aspirations for permanent migration and a future in Australia, under the guise of re-establishing the 'integrity' of Australian international education.[2] While this chapter offers an overview of the different pathways traversed by former students, Chapter 2 provides a more detailed account of what occurred when students attempted to obtain permanency through the General Skilled Migration Program.

While it is impossible to offer a conclusive account of the different directions taken by former international students targeted by these changes, one thing is clear: the changes were neither designed for expelling former international students from Australia and back to their home countries, nor did they have this effect. Rather, the raft of changes have had the dual effect of refounding the international education economy on a more sustainable footing, favouring the market share of Australian universities, whilst simultaneously creating a sizable new class of permanently provisional or overtly illegal migrants.

International education economy: A background

International students have formed a numerically and politically significant component of Australia's migration program — and, in turn, the Australian populace — since 2001, when the Coalition Government under then Prime Minister John Howard made extensive changes to the *Migration Regulations 1994* ('the *Regulations*') to permit international students to apply for a range of permanent visas on

---

2   For an account and chronology of those changes up until 2009, see Bob Birrell and Bronwen Perry, 'Immigration Policy Change and the International Student Industry' (2009) 17 *People and Place* 64.

a concessional basis.[3] Alongside the reshaping of the humanitarian program and his introduction of the Business (Long Stay) subclass 457 visa, the changes to the *Regulations* concerning overseas students are now considered to be amongst Howard's crowning immigration reforms.[4]

While under Howard international education was initially posited as a means of softening higher education funding cuts,[5] increasingly the industry's profitability was derived from the VET sector. In May 2005, the occupations of cookery and hairdressing were added to the Migration Occupations in Demand List (MODL) in a move demographer Bob Birrell drily describes as 'a decisive moment in recent immigration history'.[6]

From 2005 to 2008, while overseas student commencements in universities remained largely stable, numbers in the VET sector (subclass 572) increased by 183 per cent.[7] India and China were the two leading nationalities represented in these increased visa grants.[8] In 1996, when the Howard Coalition Government took office, there were less than 100,000 overseas students enrolled in Australian schools

3   Mary Crock and Laurie Berg, *Immigration, Refugees and Forced Migration: Law, Policy and Practice in Australia* (The Federation Press, 2011) 298–328. The 'concessional' nature of the skilled visa subclasses for international students derived from the earlier introduction in 1999 of the 'Migration Occupations in Demand List' (MODL) reflecting occupations in skills shortage, and the attribution of additional qualifying 'points' to students having completed qualifications in areas linked to the MODL. In addition, students having completed relevant qualifications in their skilled occupation in Australia were exempted from the requirement, imposed on overseas applicants, of having completed relevant work experience in their field. See Bob Birrell and Ernest Healy, 'The February 2010 Reforms and the International Student Industry' (2010) 18 (1) *People and Place* 65.
4   Peter Mares, 'The Permanent Shift to Temporary Migration' in Perera et al. (eds), *Enter at Own Risk: Australia's Population Questions for the 21st Century* (Black Swan Press, 2010) 65, 65–91.
5   Jon Stratton, 'Preserving White Hegemony: Skilled Migration, "Asians" and Middle Class Assimilation' in Perera et al. (eds), *Enter at Own Risk: Australia's Population Questions for the 21st Century* (Black Swan Press, 2010) 38, 38.
6   Bob Birrell and Ernest Healy, above fn 3, 68.
7   Bob Birrell and Bronwen Perry, above fn 2, 66.
8   Department of Immigration and Citizenship, 'Student Visa Program Trends: 2003–04 to 2009–10' (2011). Available at: www.border.gov.au/ReportsandPublications/Documents/statistics/student-visa-program-trends-2009-10.pdf; Bob Birrell and Ernest Healy, above fn 3. According to AEI figures cited by Birrell and Perry, growth in the VET sector over 2005–08 was largely attributable to Indian visa applicants, who accounted for 44 per cent of new student commencements over the period. See Bob Birrell and Bronwen Perry, above fn 2, 66.

and universities; by 2009 there were 600,000.[9] By 2011, at its peak, the international education economy cumulatively attracted $18.6 billion in export income to Australia. This made international education the third most profitable export earner, after coal and iron ore. Though described as '*export* income', the benefits of the international education economy flowed mostly to local business and communities:

> In fact, the majority (52 per cent) of the $15.7 billion revenue from international education in 2011 flowed to the host communities — the local shops and retail sector, accommodation providers, travel services and other community enterprises.[10]

In describing the growth of the international education industry from 2005 onwards, Monash University academic and famed economic nationalist[11] Bob Birrell narrates a process largely passive on the Australian side, driven entirely by the push of opportunistic agents and entrants from India fixing on the closer linkages between VET study and permanent migration outcomes. According to Birrell:

> This confluence of events gave VET providers a new and potent marketing tool in order to attract students. They found a huge pool of potential clients in Asia, particularly in the Indian Punjab, who were interested in taking up the opportunity.

Birrell's historical analysis is not only entirely mechanistic, but is obfuscatory in its categorical failure to address the multiple, active, and aggressive processes through which VET sector enrolments were courted and facilitated not only by providers but extensive Australian networks encompassing the (then) Department of Immigration and Citizenship (DIAC)[12] as well as Australian universities from 2005 onwards.

---

9   Australian Human Rights Commission, 'Principles to Promote and Protect the Human Rights of International Students' (October 2012).

10   International Education Advisory Council, 'Australia: Educating Globally' (February 2013). Available at: internationaleducation.gov.au/International-network/Australia/InternationalStrategy/theCouncilsReport/Documents/Australia%20–%20Educating.%20Globally%20FINAL%20REPORT.pdf.

11   *The Australian*, 'The Top 50: Education: Bob Birrell', 31 January 2012. Available at: www.theaustralian.com.au/top50/2012/bob-birrell/story-fnbttwrn-1226258657279.

12   Note that, on 18 September 2013, the former Department of Immigration and Citizenship was superseded by the Department of Immigration and Border Protection.

A major player in facilitating recruitment over this period was the multimillion-dollar Australian venture, IDP Education Pvt Ltd, and its international outcrops, specifically in India. IDP Education's company profile indicates that it is co-owned by 38 Australian universities, as well as Seek Ltd, a major online recruitment and training company.[13] The company's Indian-based branch, IDP India, has for years coordinated road-show-like education fairs in major Indian capitals, showcasing representatives from Australian universities, TAFEs, VET providers, and schools, regarding prospects for work and study in Australia. IDP India has been and continues to be entirely unabashed in linking study pathways in Australia with more long-term migration outcomes, as exhibited in its online promotional material for the Australian Education Fair 2013, which announces 'visa rules relaxed' and highlights new post-study work visas available to students as of right after completion of a bachelor or higher degree course.[14] In another example, the Australian High Commission in New Delhi in 2009 advertised that it 'worked closely' with a body by the name of Association of Australian Education Representatives in India (AAERI), whose purpose was to 'assure the integrity and credibility of agents who are recruiting students on behalf of Australian education and training institutions'.[15] AAERI's material presents it as a quasi-official body of education agents and advisors based in India, operating with the imprimatur of the Australian Government and DIAC, under a purported 'code of ethics' that tellingly remains entirely silent on the provision of immigration advice and assistance by agents.[16] In Australia, too, a highly profitable and entirely unregulated quasi-professional industry of 'education agents' sprung up, with loose and unarticulated links to colleges and universities, allowing them to offer students assistance with course admission and visa applications without cost, given their fees could be recuperated through agency agreements with education providers.[17]

---

13   IDP Education Pvt Ltd, *LinkedIn Company Profile*. Available at: www.linkedin.com/company/idp-education-pty-ltd.

14   IDP India, *Australian Education Fair 2013*. Available at: www.collegeadmission.in/Other%20Information/EducationalEvents/2013/IDP_Australian_Education_Fair_2013.shtml.

15   Association of Australian Education Representatives in India, *About AAERI*. Available at: www.aaeri.in/home.html.

16   Association of Australian Education Representatives in India, *Code of Ethical Practices in Agents/Representatives Offices*. Available at: www.aaeri.in/code_of_ethics.html.

17   International Student Legal Advice Clinic, 'Submission to the Senate Education, Employment and Workplace Relations Committee Inquiry into the Welfare of International Students' 8–13.

Through these means, many tens of thousands of students were corralled into courses, not only in the private VET sector, but the vocational education offshoots of major Australian universities, including the memorably named Ozford College (affiliated with Central Queensland University), and Melbourne Institute of Business and Technology (affiliated with Deakin University).[18] The precise relationships between Australian universities and VET providers varied, taking diverse forms ranging from board membership to partial ownership, and investment. Even beyond the obvious cut derived by Australia's 38 major universities from investment in IDP Education as described above, it is clear that the university sector stood in direct relation to the developing international VET sector, despite later revisionist attempts by Birrell and others to elide this relation, particularly when the VET sector came to crisis from 2008 onwards.

From 2005 onwards, with the question of enrolment significantly eased through the various relationships and processes described above, potential entrants had only to worry about the remaining visa criteria — principally, access to funds sufficient for living expenses, course fees, and travel during the visa holder's intended stay in Australia.[19] Aspiring students were able to meet these requirements variously through mortgaging ancestral property (in the case of Punjab, often representing the last of familial landholdings following the immiseration caused by the Green Revolution);[20] high-interest loans procured from agents and to be repaid by the student on arrival in Australia; or contractual arrangements with secondary visa holders (the primary applicant's 'husband' or 'wife') to demonstrate the required funds in exchange for being included in the visa application.

Driving take-up on the Indian side, specifically in Punjab, was mass poverty, particularly amongst smaller farmers shut out of the gains of the Green Revolution, and massive population growth, coupled

---

18   The Minister for Immigration published a highly useful legislative instrument (IMMI 13/027, 23 March 2013) that reveals the relationships between Australian universities and their vocational education 'partner'. The list of partner institutions includes some of Australia's leading private international colleges, including Ozford, Navitas, MIT, and Melbourne Institute of Business and Technology.

19   These requirements were imposed through the operation of Schedule 5A of the *Migration Regulations 1994* (Cth).

20   Chhabilendra Roul, *Bitter to Better Harvest: Post-Green Revolution Agricultural and Marketing Strategy for India* (Northern Book Centre, 2001) 33–50.

with an eviscerated education sector in India.[21] Suffice it to say that VET sector students who were recruited and travelled to Australia from 2005 onwards tended to represent the poorest sectors of the populations of rural India and China, and who arrived in the context of overwhelming debt and obligation to make good on the investment of their families and communities.

Some 210,888 VET sector student visas were granted to overseas applicants between 2005 and 2012. A combination of punitive visa conditions (the requirement to service ever-increasing tuition fees while being limited to working only 20 hours per week), together with the racialisation of new entrants, ensured that students rapidly came to occupy a new underclass in the labour market — disproportionately represented in cabs, service stations, convenience stores, and as labour hire for roof insulation and construction work. At the same time, the profit-seeking growth in the VET sector meant that course content and learning was nominal only: students attended cookery classes in converted CBD office buildings only to find ovens fitted without gas connections.[22] Documenting the seemingly unending growth in the international education economy in 2011, Ben Rosenzweig and Liz Thompson wrote:

> The dynamics of these economies were persistently rendered opaque by two officially-sponsored fantasies: that these economies were essentially about 'education', with the desire for migration secondary or incidental; and secondarily that all of these genuine students did not to have to work for money.[23]

---

21 David Feith, 'India's Higher Education Sector in the Twenty-First Century: A Growing Market and the Need for Greater International Engagement', paper presented at the 17th Biennial Conference of the Asian Studies Association of Australia, Melbourne (July 2008).
22 Examples of these practices abound. In a feature on SBS's *Insight* program that aired on 21 July 2009, most students studying at VET providers related similar examples. Harry Singh of Sydney, for instance, states: 'I didn't know anyone here and I didn't know about colleges. I was thinking colleges would be big like India colleges. But it's small, like a cabinet colleges. It's very small, like it's a house or it's offices, yeah. It's not like the colleges as compared to India … Yeah, in the prospectus, in the booklet, it showed Harbour Bridge, Opera House, instead of a college building, yeah and some of the college prospectus shows, like, the gate of the fort and, like a Sydney college gate and all that. They show like this.' SBS Insight, *Transcript: At Risk* (21 July 2009). Available at: www.sbs.com.au/insight/episode/transcript/87/At-Risk.
23 Liz Thompson and Ben Rosenzweig, 'Public Policy Is Class War Pursued by Other Means: Struggle and Restructuring as International Education Economy' (2011) 3 *Interface* 39, 49.

It is entirely disingenuous to ask how many students arrived in Australia over this period for the 'right reasons', or as 'genuine students', as opposed to simply seeking a pathway to more permanent settlement in Australia. It is disingenuous chiefly because the overt linking of student visas with permanent migration outcomes from 2001 onwards was precisely what contributed to increased enrolment and ensured the growth of the international education sector. There was a clear intention by the government (if not an overt promise) that students could pursue permanent migration on completion of their studies in Australia. An entire private education industry — not to mention a greatly expanded Australian university and TAFE sector — grew up in the shadow of this explicit promise.

It was this historical and political grouping of temporary entrants, forged in a very particular moment in the growth of Australia's international education economy, who could be seen on the streets of Melbourne holding signs that read, 'We don't just drive your cabs, we drive your economy'.

'The expulsion'

Throughout 2007 and 2008, Melbourne's CBD was brought to a standstill on several occasions by wildcat protests organised by the city's cab drivers. Mostly international students and (representative of the VET sector's makeup at the time) largely from the Indian subcontinent, the drivers protested the conditions of their labour and, most specifically, the unique and cruel forms of exploitation deriving from their tenuous legal status as international students. Disruptive as these protests were, they managed to gain little press and political traction. However, when largely the same people took to Flinders Street station in May 2009, organising under the banner of 'international students' and protesting the conditions of the international education economy as a whole, a furious public relations spectacle ensued between the governments of Australia and India to recover the tarnished image of the multi-billion dollar industry.[24]

---

24 Benjamin Rosenzweig, 'International Student Struggles, or, Causes of the Mediated Process of Reproduction' (2010). Available at: hutnyk.wordpress.com/2010/08/18/ben-rosenzweig-theory-of-the-offensive-blog/; Liz Thompson and Ben Rosenzweig, above fn 23.

Analyses from that period tend to attribute a certain critical force to the 2009 protests in terms of the reforms to the international education sector that followed in the years after. In my view, this reading is both unduly optimistic and insufficiently attentive to the shifts underway as the protests took place. In 2006, former immigration minister Amanda Vanstone commissioned a far-reaching evaluation into the efficacy of the MODL and skilled migration outcomes, which was largely damning of the linking of VET sector education to permanent visa pathways.[25] Bob Birrell sat on the panel of that evaluation. When the Rudd Labor Government took power in late 2007, thousands of permanent visa applications were pending from former students seeking to parlay their study into a permanent visa outcome (as promised). By December 2008, then immigration minister Chris Evans issued students with a foreboding warning, indicating that skilled visa applications by VET students whose courses were not on a select critical skills list would not be afforded processing priority and would languish in the processing pipeline for years. A strategic decision was made to leave cooking and hairdressing (the field in which several tens of thousands of students had obtained their qualifications) off the critical skills list.[26] The movement towards culling the international education sector was well underway by the time international students began to organise in 2009. What the protests did provide, however, was the convenient imagery and trope of 'crisis' in the international education sector, which lent a sense of inexorability to the drastic measures that followed.

As a result of the protests, public discussion fixed on the spectre of the 'dodgy college' as the source of the resulting clamour in the international education economy. The 'dodgy college' and 'residency factory' did the work of casting the 'crisis' in international education as an aberration, an unintended consequence, a result of external corruption as opposed to the logical and necessary conclusion of the industry's profit-seeking imperatives. At the same time, and more importantly, projecting the problems of the international education economy onto the 'dodgy colleges' gave license to the later

---

25   Bob Birrell, Lesleyanne Hawthorne and Sue Richardson, 'Evaluation of General Skilled Migration Categories Report' (Department of Immigration and Multicultural Affairs, March 2006).
26   Bob Birrell and Bronwen Perry, above fn 2.

consequences that were visited onto the attendees of those colleges — VET sector visa holders — who, by presumption, came to represent an amorphous mass of 'dodgy' international students.

The year 2010 saw the unending proliferation of changes and measures taken to reinforce the 'integrity' of the international education economy — that is, to re-establish it on an equally profitable footing less beholden to the vagaries of student protest and international censure. A spate of audits were conducted into international colleges operating throughout Melbourne, which lasted until the auditing body itself fell under scrutiny for its internal processes.[27] Enhanced 'integrity checking' led to high rates of student visa cancellations, and a massive rise in the refusal of further student visa applications by Indian and Chinese nationals in particular.[28]

In 2011, the introduction of the 'genuine student' and 'genuine temporary entrant' criteria for student visas operated as a *carte blanche* permitting the Department of Immigration to refuse further student visa applications based on an assessment of the applicant's study history — i.e. whether they were previously enrolled in the international VET sector.[29] At the same time, 'streamlined processing' arrangements were introduced for students enrolled at universities, meaning student visas could be granted without English language or financial evidence if a student could show confirmation of enrolment in a bachelor or higher course when applying for the visa.[30]

The cornerstone of the international education economy's reformation was the overnight change to the MODL on 8 February 2010, which was replaced with a new Skilled Occupations List (SOL) divided into three schedules. The effect of the 8 February 2010 changes was to limit eligibility for general skilled migration to a select number

---

27   Victorian Registration and Qualifications Authority, 'Outcomes of AUQA Higher Education Audit of VRQA', 10 *VRQA Newsletter*. Available at: www.vrqa.vic.gov.au/enews/pages/Edition-10/article1.aspx.

28   Jaswinder Sidhu, 'Discretionary Powers Target Indian Students, 49% Offshore Visa Applications Rejected', *South Asia Times*, 17 December 2012. Available at: www.southasiatimes.com.au/news/?p=3235.

29   Bernard Lane, 'Call to Rethink Student Visa Test' *The Australian*, 1 March 2013. Available at: www.theaustralian.com.au/higher-education/call-to-rethink-student-visa-test/story-e6frgcjx-1226587879775.

30   Parliament of Australia, 'Overseas students: Immigration policy changes 1997–2015' (2016). Available at: www.aph.gov.au/About_Parliament/Parliamentary_Departments/Parliamentary_Library/pubs/rp/rp1516/OverseasStudents.

of predominantly professional occupations on the pared-back SOL. The implications of these changes to the MODL are too extensive to list here, but for our purposes it is enough to say that for the 121,378 VET sector student visa holders in Australia at that time[31] — a cohort who had paid thousands for an education never obtained and who had worked the most violent and precarious jobs imaginable in the Australian economy — any hope of a permanent migration outcome was all but destroyed.

Liz Thompson and Ben Rosenzweig described that moment as 'the expulsion', in the following terms:

> The ALP federal government responded to the movements of guest consumers and to fractures in the smooth development of international education economies by sweeping a large part of these economies away and many of those on international student visas out of the country — all in one movement collapsing together economic restructuring, border control and repression. The state sought to disperse struggles and solve problems without having to acknowledge or confront anti-Indian xenophobia in particular or broader hostility to non-white non-citizens, largely by acting to dispense with a section of the (particularly private) international education industry, and with a section of the (particularly less wealthy and/or more likely to be troublesome) students ... The restructuring of these economies was thus configured as a reassertion of labour market management as well as a defence of the 'integrity' of the immigration and border control apparatuses of the Australian state — a performance of sovereignty proudly evoking that readiness for violence the possibility of which seeks to ritually re-found state and nation.[32]

However, my contention is that talk of 'expulsion' of former international students has been both premature and misconceived. After all, the logic of the border is not exclusively to halt movement but rather to sort, redirect and modulate its forms in ways ultimately productive of new segments in the labour market — to funnel movement into value and, inasmuch, redraw the lines of the nation across social relations.[33]

---

31 These statistics are taken from the closest recorded month to the changes: December 2009.

32 Liz Thompson and Ben Rosenzweig, above fn 23, 68.

33 Angela Mitropoulos, *From Precariousness to Risk Management and Beyond* (European Institute for Progressive Cultural Policies, 2011). Available at: eipcp.net/transversal/0811/mitropoulos/en.

Dispersal

Nicholas De Genova speaks of the spectre of migrant 'illegality' and the public spectacle of exclusion and expulsion as laying the symbolic groundwork for the subordinated inclusion of migrant workers into the national populace, in a manner that is particularly useful and apt to understanding the situation of VET sector students from 2010 onwards.[34] The constantly reiterated and enacted discourses of exclusion and expulsion, according to De Genova, lend migrant 'illegality' a semblance of fact, attributing it to some primordial or pre-existing quality of the migrants themselves, as opposed to the changing relations of the migrant to the state.

However, the result of performances of 'illegality' and exclusion is not necessarily to exclude or expel, but to set the scene for a particularly mediated form of inclusion:

> And yet, the more that the Border Spectacle generates anti-immigrant controversy, the more that the veritable inclusion of those targeted for exclusion proceeds apace. The 'inclusion' of those deportable migrants, of course, is finally devoted to the subordination of their labour, which can be best accomplished only to the extent that their incorporation is permanently beleaguered with the kinds of exclusionary and commonly racist campaigns that ensure that this inclusion is itself, precisely, a form of subjugation. What is at stake, then, is a larger sociopolitical (and legal) process of inclusion through exclusion, labour importation (whether overt or covert) premised upon protracted deportability.[35]

On one reading, the 2010 changes to the international education sector enacted a moment of exclusion that shifted the burden of 'illegality' of VET sector students from the state and onto themselves. And yet, the subordinated inclusion of former VET sector students proceeds apace. The 122,149 former VET sector students, and probably thousands more affected by the migration reforms of 2010 onwards, have dispersed so far as we can recognise in a number of disparate directions, depending on their cache of skills and social capital. Beyond the various pathways discussed below, Chapter 2 focuses on the permanent state of limbo

---

34   Nicholas De Genova, 'Spectacles of Migrant "Illegality": The Scene of Exclusion, the Obscene of Inclusion' (2013) 36(7) *Ethnic and Racial Studies* 1180.
35   Ibid., 1185–6.

experienced by students who applied for permanent residency through the General Skilled Migration Program, only to find their applications afforded the lowest level of priority according to the Department of Immigration's newly introduced directives.

Transitional arrangements

The changes to the general skilled migration rules on 8 February 2010 offered students an out in the form of transitional arrangements allowing persons who held a student visa on 8 February 2010 to apply for an 18-month Skilled (Graduate)(Temporary) Visa, based on the more extensive SOL that included several trade occupations.[36] The subclass 485 visa was introduced by the Coalition Government in 2007 as a 'concession' to the international education industry in exchange for tightening the English language requirements for skilled migration.[37]

While it only offers students a further 18 months in Australia, nonetheless, the path to a subclass 485 visa has proven precarious.

In April 2011, the *Regulations* were amended to introduce a new 'Public Interest Criterion' (PIC) 4020, designed to disqualify applications containing fraudulent or misleading information, or bogus documents.[38] PIC 4020 has been applied in a notably harsh manner to further visa applications by former VET students, including subclass 485 applications. In a 2012 Migration Review Tribunal decision, the review applicant, a former subclass 572 visa holder and cookery student, had his subclass 485 application refused at the primary stage by application of PIC 4020, for having presented a bogus document.[39] The bogus document was alleged to be a work experience letter from his former employer, Tandoori Lounge. The allegation that the reference was bogus arose from a DIAC site visit in which another employee failed to recognise a photograph of the review applicant, which had been taken from an old passport used by the applicant to enter Australia.

---

36   Department of Immigration and Citizenship, *Visa Options: Transitional Arrangements*. Available at: www.immi.gov.au/skilled/generalskilled-migration/transitional/ (site discontinued).
37   Bob Birrell and Ernest Healy, above fn 3.
38   See Department of Immigration and Citizenship, *Public Interest Criterion 4020*. Available at: www.immi.gov.au/legislation/amendments/2011/110402/lc02042011-01.htm (site discontinued).
39   See MRTA 2732 (18 September 2012), specifically [21] to [24].

Many thousands of VET sector students have either taken the road to nowhere option offered by the subclass 485 visa after February 2010, or are grappling with obstacles on the way there.

Further student visas

Part of the refounding of the international education economy from 2010 onwards involved offering 'streamlined processing' of student visas for those enrolled in bachelor or higher courses.[40] While allowing universities their share of export income, these arrangements also allowed for the continuation of business as usual for former international colleges, either through new partnerships with universities — usually to offer English Language Intensive Courses for Overseas Students (ELICOS) or foundational courses[41] — or (as is the case with VU Sydney) through rebranding as university adjuncts at significant cost.[42]

Streamlined processing changes arose from a review of the student visa program conducted by former Justice Michael Knight,[43] which also recommended the introduction of automatic 'post-study work visas' of 18 months or more for students completing higher education courses.[44] The option of further study was made palatable for former students through the relative ease represented by streamlined processing, along with the possibility of automatic work rights.

Like the subclass 485 visa, the path to a further student visa has ultimately proven precarious. Amongst the Knight Review recommendations taken up with greatest speed,[45] in November 2011 new criteria were introduced to the assessment of student visa applications, under the name of the 'genuine student' and 'genuine

---

40   Universities Australia, 'Knight Review a Boon to Higher Education' (Media Release, 22 September 2011). Available at: www.universitiesaustralia.edu.au/Article Documents/406/1811%20Knight%20Review%20a%20boon%20to%20higher%20education. pdf.aspx.

41   In this respect, see the list of universities and 'partner institutions' set out in the legislative instrument of eligible providers for streamlined processing, above fn 17.

42   Victoria University Sydney is a joint venture of Victoria University and the private education provider Education Centre of Australia.

43   See Michael Knight, 'Strategic Review of the Student Visa Program 2011' (Report to the Australian Government, June 2011) Recommendation 3. Available at: www.border.gov.au/ ReportsandPublications/Documents/reviews-and-inquiries/2011-knight-review.pdf.

44   See ibid., Recommendation 4.

45   See ibid., Recommendations 1–2.

temporary entrant' criteria. Ministerial Direction 53 guiding the application of those criteria specifically drew the decision-maker's attention to factors affecting former VET sector students, including 'circumstances in their home country' (i.e. poverty) and 'previous study history' (i.e. 'whether the applicant has undertaken a series of short, inexpensive courses').[46]

The operation of the 'genuine temporary entrant' criterion in screening out applicants of particular nationalities was evident in the case of offshore student visa refusal rates in India. Over 2010 to 2011, the rate of approval for student visa applications from India fell from around 90.8 per cent to only 49.6 per cent, attributed largely to applicants' failure to meet 'genuine temporary entrant' requirements.[47] The effects were also felt onshore. In the 2010–11 and 2012–13 reporting periods, student visa refusals constituted the highest number of review applications lodged with the Migration Review Tribunal.[48] Several thousand former students now exist in legal limbo, sometimes waiting years for their cases to be constituted by the tribunal, holding bridging visas in the meantime with limited or no work rights.

Employer-sponsored options

Provided that they were able to find a willing employer, the Business (Long Stay) subclass 457 visa remained an available option for skilled former VET sector students. Until July 2013, the list of occupations for which an applicant could nominate under subclass 457 visa included a healthy number of trades, including, importantly, cook and hairdresser.[49] Until 1 July 2012, the English language requirements also remained favourable, requiring applicants to demonstrate a test score of five on each component of the International English

---

46   See Minister for Immigration and Citizenship, 'Direction No 53: Assessing the Genuine Temporary Entrant Criterion for Student Visa Applications'. Available at: immi-to-australia.com/pdf/imm4_6.pdf.

47   FactCheck, 'Christopher Pyne Exaggerates Labor's International Student "Failure"', *ABC*, 11 October 2013. Available at: www.abc.net.au/news/2013-10-04/pyne-international-student-failure/4994330.

48   Migration Review Tribunal and Refugee Review Tribunal, 'MRT–RRT Caseload Report 30 June 2011' (2011); Migration Review Tribunal and Refugee Review Tribunal, 'Annual Report 2012–2013' (2013).

49   See Legislative Instrument IMMI 09/125, 'Specification of Occupations (Subparagraphs 2.72(10)(a) and 2.72I(5)(b)' 26 October 2009.

Language Testing System (IELTS) test, and including exemptions to this requirement. In the immediate aftermath of the February 2010 changes, however, the greatest difficulty with the subclass 457 visa pathway for VET students was the requirement for sponsors to pay above the Temporary Skilled Migration Income Threshold (which in 2010 amounted to $45,222 a year) and equivalent market salary rates. While for some trade occupations this base was well within market rates, for cooks and hairdressers it was significantly above award rates and was more than employers would have been willing to pay for graduates from the maligned international VET sector.[50]

Perhaps symptomatic of this are allegations that former Singapore Oil CEO Eddie Kang extracted hundreds of thousands of dollars from several hundred former international students on the promise of securing sponsorship for subclass 457 visas.[51] Specifically affected were numerous VET qualified cooks and hairdressers.[52]

Migration/refugee review tribunals

Throughout the program years 2010–11 and 2012–13, student visa refusals and cancellations constituted by far the highest rate of lodgements in the Migration Review Tribunal.[53] During that period, the tribunal's online services indicated a wait period of around two years for a review hearing and decision for these cases.

Similarly, in 2010–11, China and India constituted by far the highest rate of lodgements in the Refugee Review Tribunal in relation to Protection Visa refusals. As set out above, these two national groups were also the highest represented in VET sector student visa grants from 2005 onwards,[54] and thus most liable to be impacted by the 2010 changes. During the 2010–11 financial year, 689 applications were lodged in the Refugee Review Tribunal by Chinese nationals, and

---

50   Bob Birrell and Ernest Healy, above fn 3, 79.

51   Steve Cannane, 'Sydney Businessman Eddie Kang Accused of Ripping Off Foreign Students Over 457 Visa Contracts', *ABC Lateline*, 15 October 2013. Available at: www.abc.net.au/news/2013-10-15/sydney-businessman-accused-in-alleged-visa-rort/5022152.

52   Ibid.

53   In the 2010–11 reporting year, student visa refusals and cancellations constituted 41 per cent of lodgements in the Migration Review Tribunal; in 2012–13 they constituted 35 per cent of lodgements. See Migration Review Tribunal and Refugee Review Tribunal, above fn 48.

54   See Department of Immigration and Citizenship, above fn 8.

435 by Indian nationals — which represented a 97 per cent rise in lodgements from India.[55] At the same time, the tribunal still had 477 visa applications on hand to decide from the previous year.[56]

Former students may have more or less success in their review applications at the Migration Review Tribunal or Refugee Review Tribunal. In any case, it remains a provisional strategy for prolonging stay in Australia.

Illegality

Former VET sector students have found other options, particularly in the form of other employer- or partner-sponsored visas. The final and most obvious option is illegality, simply staying on in the country without any formal or legal status. Discussions of illegality and its consequences have not been prevalent in Australia, as compared with Europe and North America, whose geographic landscapes permit for mass undocumented entry.

What is salient in discussions of illegality is that there is nothing *irregular* about irregular migration and undocumented migrants forming an indispensable part of the labour market in both contexts.

Australia has not historically had the benefit of a sizable flow of flexible labour without status, with all the opportunities for exploitation that this implies. Former student visa holders are slowly shifting into the permanently illegal communities of regional Victoria, working alongside Samoan and Fijian former seasonal workers, and offshore entry protection visa applicants released into the community on bridging E visas.

What are the social implications of creating a permanently illegal class of residents, without the entitlements to education, welfare, medical care, and social recognition that legal status implies? What will these communities look like five or 10 years into the future, and what impact will their existence bring to the future direction of migration policy?

---

55   Ibid.
56   Ibid.

These questions, of course, cannot be answered in advance of people's movements and attempts at contestation. What I have sought to pose here is the question, not of the consequences of expulsion, but the forms of differential inclusion of those formerly holding VET sector visas — not as a long-past historical quandary, but a present social process in the unfolding.

Bibliography

Association of Australian Education Representatives in India, *About AAERI*. Available at: www.aaeri.in/home.html

Association of Australian Education Representatives in India, *Code of Ethical Practices in Agents/Representatives Offices*. Available at: www.aaeri.in/code_of_ethics.html

The Australian, 'The Top 50: Education: Bob Birrell', 31 January 2012. Available at: www.theaustralian.com.au/top50/2012/bob-birrell/story-fnbttwrn-1226258657279

Australian Education International, 'Research Snapshot: Export Income to Australia from Education Services 2010–2011' (November 2011). Available at: www.aei.gov.au/research/Research-Snapshots/Documents/Export%20Income%202010-11.pdf (site discontinued)

Australian Human Rights Commission, 'Principles to Promote and Protect the Human Rights of International Students' (October 2012)

Birrell, Bob, Lesleyanne Hawthorne and Sue Richardson, 'Evaluation of General Skilled Migration Categories Report' (Department of Immigration and Multicultural Affairs, March 2006)

Birrell, Bob and Ernest Healy, 'The February 2010 Reforms and the International Student Industry' (2010) 18 *People and Place* 65

Birrell, Bob and Bronwen Perry, 'Immigration Policy Change and the International Student Industry' (2009) 17 *People and Place* 64

Cannane, Steve, 'Sydney Businessman Eddie Kang Accused of Ripping Off Foreign Students Over 457 Visa Contracts', *ABC Lateline*, 15 October 2013. Available at: www.abc.net.au/news/2013-10-15/sydney-businessman-accused-in-alleged-visa-rort/5022152

Crock, Mary and Laurie Berg, *Immigration, Refugees and Forced Migration: Law, Policy and Practice in Australia* (The Federation Press, 2011)

De Genova, Nicholas, 'Spectacles of Migrant "Illegality": The Scene of Exclusion, the Obscene of Inclusion' (2013) 36 *Ethnic and Racial Studies* 1180

Department of Immigration and Citizenship, *Public Interest Criterion 4020*. Available at: www.immi.gov.au/legislation/amendments/2011/110402/lc02042011-01.htm (site discontinued)

Department of Immigration and Citizenship, *Visa Options: Transitional Arrangements*. Available at: www.immi.gov.au/skilled/general-skilled-migration/transitional/ (site discontinued)

Department of Immigration and Citizenship, 'Student Visa Program Trends: 2003–04 to 2009–10' (2011). Available at: www.border.gov.au/ReportsandPublications/Documents/statistics/student-visa-program-trends-2009-10.pdf

FactCheck, 'Christopher Pyne Exaggerates Labor's International Student "Failure"', *ABC,* 11 October 2013. Available at: www.abc.net.au/news/2013-10-04/pyne-international-student-failure/4994330

Feith, David, 'India's Higher Education Sector in the Twenty-First Century: A Growing Market and the Need for Greater International Engagement', paper presented at the 17th Biennial Conference of the Asian Studies Association of Australia, Melbourne (July 2008)

IDP Education Pvt Ltd, *LinkedIn Company Profile*. Available at: www.linkedin.com/company/idp-education-pty-ltd

IDP India, *Australian Education Fair 2013*. Available at: www.collegeadmission.in/Other%20Information/Educational Events/2013/IDP_Australian_Education_Fair_2013.shtml

International Education Advisory Council, 'Australia: Educating Globally' (February 2013). Available at: internationaleducation.gov.au/International-network/Australia/InternationalStrategy/theCouncilsReport/Documents/Australia%20–%20Educating%20Globally%20FINAL%20REPORT.pdf

International Student Legal Advice Clinic, 'Submission to the Senate Education, Employment and Workplace Relations Committee: Inquiry into the Welfare of International Students' (August 2009)

Knight, Michael, 'Strategic Review of the Student Visa Program 2011' (Report to the Australian Government, June 2011). Available at: www.border.gov.au/ReportsandPublications/Documents/reviews-and-inquiries/2011-knight-review.pdf

Lane, Bernard, 'Call to Rethink Student Visa Test', *The Australian*, 1 March 2013. Available at: www.theaustralian.com.au/higher-education/call-to-rethink-student-visa-test/story-e6frgcjx-1226587879775

Mares, Peter, 'The Permanent Shift to Temporary Migration' in Perera et al. (eds), *Enter at Own Risk: Australia's Population Questions for the 21st Century* (Black Swan Press, 2010) 65

Migration Review Tribunal and Refugee Review Tribunal, 'Annual Report 2012–2013' (2013)

Migration Review Tribunal and Refugee Review Tribunal, 'MRT–RRT Caseload Report 30 June 2011' (2011)

Minister for Immigration and Citizenship, 'Direction No 53: Assessing the Genuine Temporary Entrant Criterion for Student Visa Applications'. Available at: immi-to-australia.com/pdf/imm4_6.pdf

Mitropoulos, Angela, *From Precariousness to Risk Management and Beyond* (European Institute for Progressive Cultural Policies, 2011). Available at: eipcp.net/transversal/0811/mitropoulos/en

Parliament of Australia, 'Overseas students: Immigration policy changes 1997–2015' (2016). Available at: www.aph.gov.au/About_Parliament/Parliamentary_Departments/Parliamentary_Library/pubs/rp/rp1516/OverseasStudents

Rosenzweig, Benjamin, 'International Student Struggles, Or, Causes of the Mediated Process of Reproduction'. Available at: hutnyk.wordpress.com/2010/08/18/ben-rosenzweig-theory-of-the-offensive-blog/

Roul, Chhabilendra, *Bitter to Better Harvest: Post-Green Revolution Agricultural and Marketing Strategy for India* (Northern Book Centre, 2001)

SBS Insight, *Transcript: At Risk* (21 July 2009). Available at: www.sbs.com.au/insight/episode/transcript/87/At-Risk

Sidhu, Jaswinder, 'Discretionary Powers Target Indian Students, 49% Offshore Visa Applications Rejected', *South Asia Times*, 17 December 2012. Available at: www.southasiatimes.com.au/news/?p=3235

Stratton, Jon, 'Preserving White Hegemony: Skilled Migration, "Asians" and Middle Class Assimilation' in Perera et al. (eds), *Enter at Own Risk: Australia's Population Questions for the 21st Century* (Black Swan Press, 2010) 38

Thompson, Liz and Ben Rosenzweig, 'Public Policy Is Class War Pursued by Other Means: Struggle and Restructuring as International Education Economy' (2011) 3 *Interface* 39

Universities Australia, 'Knight Review a Boon to Higher Education' (Media Release, 22 September 2011). Available at: www.universitiesaustralia.edu.au/ArticleDocuments/406/1811%20Knight%20Review%20a%20boon%20to%20higher%20education.pdf.aspx

Victorian Registration and Qualifications Authority, 'Outcomes of AUQA Higher Education Audit of VRQA', 10 *VRQA Newsletter*. Available at: www.vrqa.vic.gov.au/enews/pages/Edition-10/article1.aspx

2

Great Expectations and the Twilight Zone: The Human Consequences of the Linking of Australia's International Student and Skilled Migration Programs and the Dismantling of that Scheme

Sudrishti Reich

Introduction

In the early to mid-2000s, an explicit government policy was developed to expand Australia's share of the lucrative and competitive international education market. A legitimate pathway was created from student status to permanent residence status. This scheme, intended to entice more foreign students and provide a source of locally trained young skilled migrants, was on one level hugely successful. It led to a massive and sustained increase in international student numbers. However, the policy was also, eventually, hugely damaging. It was damaging to the perceived effectiveness of the skilled migration program, and, ironically, to the international education industry it had been designed (in part) to assist. On a human level, when the scheme was dismantled, it was most damaging to thousands of former students who had invested, in good faith, in an Australian education and the prospect of becoming Australian permanent residents.

This chapter tracks and examines the sequence of immigration policy changes made in the student and skilled migration programs over the decade beginning in 2001, and explores their intended and unintended consequences. Most importantly, it focuses on and analyses the consequences for the thousands of former students whose lives were affected by the rapid dismantling of the government's policy of linking student visas with a migration outcome.

The first sequence of policy changes created a nexus between holding a student visa and becoming eligible for permanent skilled migration. Ultimately, the scheme provided for international students who had successfully completed their Australian qualifications in occupations considered to be in demand to satisfy the criteria for the grant of a permanent visa under the skilled migration program. As will be described, by mid-decade, the interrelationship between the student and skilled migration programs had begun to result in unintended and untenable consequences. The policies led to a boom in international student enrolments, particularly in the VET (Vocational Education and Training) sector, and a blow out in the number of applications for permanent skilled visas — which eventually exceeded the annual quota and created a pipeline of applications. Relying on the legislative pathway, increasing numbers of students applied to stay on permanently in Australia after completing their studies. Additionally, the policies resulted in an over-representation of certain occupations offered by skilled visa applicants, which, in the view of government, no longer reflected the skill needs of Australia nor served its economic interests. As a result of these cumulative consequences, a further series of policy changes were implemented that eventually de-linked the two components of the migration program.

This chapter describes how a reactive over-compensation to the outcomes of policy settings linking study in Australia with eligibility for permanent skilled migration left thousands of former international students languishing for years in a twilight zone of precarious temporary status. In doing so, it attempts to make visible this particular period in Australia's immigration history during which a sequence of policies were implemented in reaction to unfolding unintended consequences of previous policies, ostensibly in the national interest, yet with devastating consequences for a large group of former students. It analyses the effects of the policy reversal on these students/visa applicants and questions what lessons may be learned from this experience. These students were deliberately encouraged by government policy to choose Australia as their study destination by the offer of the possibility of transitioning to permanent residence. Having had their legitimate expectations raised, the laws were changed and visa processing priorities were adjusted, and their pathway to permanent residence was effectively blocked. This large cohort of disenfranchised applicants was left in an immigration no-man's land — not legitimate temporary workers, nor permanent residents, but instead permanent visa applicants. They have been left for years as temporary bridging visa[1] holders, excluded from the rights and security of permanent residence status, despite having invested years of their lives in Australia. As permanent visa applicants holding bridging visas, they struggle to secure skilled employment and are rapidly de-skilling — forced into low-skilled, low-paid labour, and vulnerable to exploitation. In this process, their ability to contribute fully to the society they have chosen to join is being undermined. Yet, financially and socially, the price of going home without permanent residence is too high.

The picture is put together by examining the series of policy and legislative changes introduced over a decade; analysing the public policy statements (such as media releases and speeches) of government ministers throughout the period; referencing reports on the international education sector and media coverage of the policy shifts and their consequences; collating statistical data and policy documents from Australian Government websites; and drawing on the personal testimony of affected former students as published on a website established by and for the so-called G4/5rs.

---

1   A bridging visa is a temporary visa granted to a person who applies for a substantive visa. Its function is to give the bridging visa holder lawful status (permission to stay in Australia) during the processing of their substantive visa application.

The creation of a pathway from student to permanent resident status

Three phases can be identified in Australia's relationship to international students.[2]

From the 1950s, under the Colombo Plan,[3] it took the form of a foreign aid program that offered stipends to promising foreign students. These students, having gained their degrees and been exposed to Australian values, culture, and society, would take their newly acquired knowledge and skills back home and contribute to the growth and development of their country.

From the 1980s there was a fundamental shift 'from aid to trade' — a market-based approach where Australia sold education to paying students. Having paid for their education, foreign students were generally not permitted under the migration laws to remain in Australia after completing their studies.

A third phase emerged at the start of the 2000s when the potential value to Australia of international students and their retention began to be realised. This phase was marked by international students being regarded as the solution to internal problems of increasing skills shortages and an ageing population.[4] In a bid to boost Australia's share of the competitive international education industry, from 2001, gradual, cumulative changes to both the student visa program and the General Skilled Migration (GSM) program brought about an explicit link between studying in Australia and obtaining permanent residency. For the first time, eligible overseas students, upon successful completion of their studies, were able to apply onshore for permanent residency through the Skilled–Independent (and Skilled–Australian-sponsored) visa categories of the GSM program.[5] A direct pathway

---

2   See, for example, Eric Meadows, 'From Aid to Industry: A History of International Education in Australia' in Dorothy Davis and Bruce Mackintosh (eds), *Making a Difference: Australian International Education* (UNSW Press, 2011) 50.

3   The Colombo Plan for Cooperative Economic Development in South and Southeast Asia — a scheme for bilateral aid for developing countries in South and Southeast Asia arising out of a meeting of Commonwealth Foreign Ministers held in Colombo, Ceylon, in January 1950.

4   See, for example, Elsa Koleth, 'Overseas Students: Immigration Policy Changes 1997–May 2010' (Background Note, Parliamentary Library, 18 June 2010).

5   See *Migration Regulations 1994* (Cth) sch 2 Visa subclass 880 Skilled–Independent Overseas Student and Visa subclass 881 Skilled–Australian-Sponsored Overseas Student.

from holding a student visa to being granted a skilled permanent visa was established. In a win–win for Australia, overseas students became a source of young, acculturised, skilled workers who had paid for their own education.

In a series of further policy and legislative changes, this pathway was steadily widened. In April 2005, the Migration Occupations in Demand List (MODL) (an essential aspect of the skilled migration points system) was amended to include additional trade occupations, including cooks and hairdressers. The list was expanded further in both 2006 and 2007, incorporating more trade occupations. A trade qualification could be obtained within the two-year minimum period of study in Australia needed to qualify for a GSM visa. For applicants who were motivated by the prospect of applying for permanent residence, choosing a trade occupation (as opposed to a tertiary qualification) was a fast route.

At the same time, the skilled visa criteria were changed so that former students who applied within six months of being awarded their Australian qualification were exempt from the usual requirement of having some years of relevant skilled work experience.[6] The combined effect of these legislative adjustments was to create a scheme whereby, by selecting a course of study that qualified an individual for one of the occupations on the MODL or that gained 60 points on the Skilled Occupations List (SOL), an international student was almost assured of becoming eligible for a permanent residence visa.[7]

The scheme effected a change to the landscape of the international student sector and the skilled migration program. From one perspective, the policy was extraordinarily successful — it led to a massive boost to international student enrolments in Australian educational institutions. There was a rapid rise in student numbers across all sectors, and a numbers explosion in the VET sector.[8] In 2005, (when the new trades were added to the MODL), there were 66,086 VET sector enrolments. Two years later in 2007, that number had

---

6   Ibid. See also *Migration Regulations 1994* (Cth) sch 2 cl 136.21.

7   The arrangement is described further in Michael Knight, 'Strategic Review of the Student Visa Program 2011' (Report to the Australian Government, June 2011) 14. Available at: www.border.gov. au/ReportsandPublications/Documents/reviews-and-inquiries/2011-knight-review.pdf.

8   It is within this context of massive demand for VET courses that some of the damaging consequences of the scheme took shape. See Chapter 1, where Verma describes the consequential breakdown of the integrity of the international education industry.

doubled. By 2009 it had almost doubled again.[9] This phenomenon can be attributed directly to the expansion of the trade occupations included in the MODL list in 2005. By 2009, international education services had become Australia's largest service export industry, contributing $18.6 billion to the economy.[10]

A feature of the boom was the changing profile of the source countries of the new students. The most dramatic change was the place taken by India. In just three years, between 2002 and 2005, India rose through the ranks of the top 10 source countries from ninth position to second, behind China, where it has remained since, despite the rapid drop off of new enrolments from India in 2009–10.[11] In the five years from 2004–09 there was a six-fold increase in the number of Indian students enrolling (from 20,500 in 2004 to 120,000 in 2009).[12]

Importantly, there was also a change in the demographic of the students coming from India. The prospect of being able to convert an Australian qualification into permanent residency provided the incentive and the opportunity for a different class of young people to apply for international student visas. Indian students entering during the mid to late 2000s were no longer only the sons and daughters of India's elite, but now included the children of families from poorer socioeconomic groups, from rural and regional areas, and lower stratums of society.[13] This new cohort has been described in a report of the Australia India Institute:

> Many of the students were children of middle class, semi-rural parents who were not just leaving India for the first time, but had never left their home states … There were other poignant aspects to their stories … parents had borrowed money from private money-lenders at high rates of interest to fund their education. The expectation was that a good degree or diploma would lead to a work permit, facilitating

---

9   Figures from Australian Education International, *International Student Data*. Available at: internationaleducation.gov.au/research/International-Student-Data/Pages/default.aspx.

10   Australian Education International, 'Research Snapshot, Export Income to Australia from Education Services in 2009' (2010). Available at: www.aei.gov.au/research/Research-Snapshots/Documents/Export%20Income%202009-10.pdf (site discontinued).

11   Figures from Australian Education International, above fn 9.

12   Ibid.

13   See Supriya Sing and Anuja Cabraal, 'Indian Student Migrants in Australia: Issues of Community Sustainability' (2010) 18 *People and Place* 25; Michiel Baas, 'Students of Migration: Indian Overseas Students and the Question of Permanent Residency' (2006) 14 *People and Place* 11.

migration and citizenship. This was a reflection of the belief that Australia was a land of opportunity and merit, and that hard work, following an initial investment, would be rewarded there.[14]

The significance of this new type of overseas student was that, coming from lower socioeconomic backgrounds, there was much more at stake in achieving a migration outcome from the choice to study in Australia. This made them more vulnerable when the scheme was eventually dismantled.

In dependence on the scheme, increasing numbers of former students chose to convert their Australian qualifications into permanent residency by applying for skilled migration in Australia. This resulted in a significant change to the pattern of visa applications in the skilled migration program. The percentage of onshore applications increased rapidly and included greater numbers of former students. In fact, the numbers of applications being received by the end of 2009 exceeded the numbers of visas available for grant in that financial year. By 2009, approximately one third of students stayed on after completing their studies and applied for permanent residence.[15] For the three to four years leading up to 2010, when the government reversed the policy, international students were the single largest contributor to Australia's net migration.[16] There was an accompanying skewing of the skilled migration program with the pool of applicants dominated by a handful of occupations — for instance, a disproportionate number of cooks, hairdressers, IT professionals, and accountants.[17] As critiqued in the Knight Review of the Student Visa Program: 'Instead of driving an increase in particular skills which Australia needed, the scheme … ended up driving migration per se.'[18]

---

14   John McCarthy et al., 'Perceptions Taskforce Beyond the Lost Decade' (Report of the Australia India Institute, 2012).

15   Dorothy Davis and Bruce Mackintosh (eds), *Making a Difference: Australian International Education* (UNSW Press, 2011) 403.

16   Chris Evans, Minister for Immigration and Citizenship, 'Changes to Australia's Skilled Migration Program' (Speech delivered at The Australian National University, Canberra, 8 February 2010).

17   Ibid.

18   Michael Knight, above fn 7, 15.

The government reaction: Reversal of policy and retraction of hope

By the beginning of 2009, the rising flood of onshore skilled visa applications and the imbalance in the occupational skills offered by the applicants coincided with the arrival of the global financial crisis in Australia. The government responded by cutting the intake of skilled migrants. It also began a process of reforming the skilled migration program, which included prioritising visa applications from applicants with an Australian employer or state sponsor. By this means, the program was designed to be more demand driven as opposed to supply driven. It sought to address the problem of a backlog of skilled visa applications by cancelling 20,000 offshore GSM visa applications lodged before 1 September 2007.[19]

The government also moved quickly, through a sequence of legislative adjustments, to dismantle the scheme linking student status and permanent residence. In February 2010, the MODL was revoked with immediate effect. Since having an occupation on the MODL enhanced an applicant's ability to achieve a pass score on the points test, its revocation meant that many students would no longer be eligible for a permanent skilled visa. In May 2010, a new Skilled Occupation List (SOL) was announced to apply from July 2010. The new SOL halved the number of eligible occupations. Critically, the new SOL omitted the occupations of cook and hairdresser. From July 2011, a new points test commenced that gave greater weight to skilled work experience and English language ability. While existing students whose occupations were on the new SOL could still apply for permanent residence, the newly focused points test, particularly on skilled work experience, largely disenfranchised most former student applicants. The extent of the government's reaction to the perceived problem of the effects of the student to permanent resident scheme was demonstrated in the introduction of a bill to give the minister the power to cap the number of visas granted to applicants in any one occupation.[20] If passed, this would have ceased certain already lodged visa applications from former

---

19   Chris Evans, Minister for Immigration and Citizenship, 'Migration Reforms to Deliver Australia's Skills Needs' (Media Release, 8 February 2010).
20   Ibid.; Migration Amendment (Visa Capping) Bill 2010.

students onshore. In the event, however, parliament was prorogued for a general election before the bill could be voted on and it has not been re-presented.

The strategy that probably had the most damaging effect on existing visa applicants was the introduction, from 1 January 2009, of priority processing directions by the Minister for Immigration. These binding directions established the order in which applications in the skilled migration program should be processed. Under these directions, applications were no longer assessed in the order in which they were lodged. Rather, priority was given to applicants who suited Australia's perceived economic needs. The processing priorities since 1 July 2012 are, in descending order:

1. applications from people who are sponsored under the Regional Sponsored Migration Scheme (RSMS) program,
2. applications from people who are sponsored under the Employer Nomination Scheme (ENS) program,
3. applications from people who are nominated by a state or territory government agency [for an occupation specified on that agency's State Migration Plan],
4. applications from people who have nominated an occupation on the Skilled Occupation List (SOL) — Schedule 1 in effect from 1 July 2012,
5. all other applications.[21]

The effect of priority processing is that those without an employer or government sponsor are always being pushed to the back of the queue as new applications from sponsored applicants are processed first. In addition, applicants invited under the SkillSelect scheme (introduced in mid-2012) are given priority within each of the priority categories.

It is important to remember that the pathway from student to permanent resident was legitimate. It was a deliberate government strategy to entice more international students to choose Australia.

---

21   Department of Immigration and Citizenship, *Fact Sheet 24a: Priority Processing for Skilled Migration Visas* (July 2012). Available at: www.immi.gov.au/media/fact-sheets/24apriority_skilled.htm (site discontinued).

This was reflected even in the government's official website for international students, *Study in Australia*. Under the heading, 'Employment: Your future. Your world', the site included the statement:

> The Australian Government skilled migration program targets young people who have skills, an education and outstanding abilities that will contribute to the Australian economy. International students with Australian qualifications account for about half the people assessed under the skilled migrant program.

It went on to give a link to the Department of Immigration website.[22]

Yet in the minister's announcements of the various policy reversals, the government went so far as to seek to blame the overseas students for relying on the laws. In the words of Chris Evans, the Minister for Immigration at the time:

> Students come here; they're coming to buy an education, not to buy a visa.[23]

> The government recognises that the changes will affect some overseas students currently in Australia intending to apply for permanent residence ... The changes will in no way impact on international students coming to Australia to gain a legitimate qualification and then return home.[24]

> The changes also remove incentives for international students to seek permanent residence through low quality education courses, a practice that damaged the integrity of both the migration program and the education industry.[25]

A statement included at the end of the Department of Immigration's information sheet on allocation of priority group five applications says: 'Many priority group 5 applicants still face a considerable wait until their application is allocated to a case officer for processing *and*

---

22   Web archive, *Study in Australia Website*. Available at: web.archive.org/web/20070620161512/www.studyinaustralia.gov.au/Sia/en/AfterYourStudies/Employment.
23   Chris Evans, Minister for Immigration and Citizenship, 'New Skilled Occupation List to Meet Australia's Economic Needs' (Media Release, 17 May 2010).
24   Ibid.
25   Chris Evans, Minister for Immigration and Citizenship, 'Australia Continues to Welcome International Students' (Media Release, 8 September 2010).

may wish to consider other options [emphasis added].'[26] As there are no comparable permanent visa options that most in this group would be eligible for, the irresistible impression of this statement is that the government hopes that this embarrassing group of visa applicants will finally despair, give up, and leave Australia. However, another co-existent possibility may be that asserted by Sanmati Verma in Chapter 1, namely that, rather than intending to expel these former students, their existence in Australia created a new class of permanently provisional migrants, providing a useful pool of subordinated and flexible labour.

Life in the twilight zone

Priority processing has had a direct impact on the prospects of the vast majority of former student applicants who have applied in the independent stream and come within priority group five (PG5).

Technically, while the policy and legislative changes were not retrospective, in their effect they were. They altered the future prospects of thousands of students who were already studying in Australia. Many would realistically no longer be eligible for a GSM visa. Others faced an indefinite state of limbo, stuck in PG5, with any higher-priority applicant entering the system being processed ahead of them. These were students who had invested tens of thousands of dollars to study in Australia.

There were transitional provisions but these only offered students the possibility of obtaining an 18-month temporary work visa at the end of their studies. This would, if they were lucky, 'enable them to ... acquire work experience and seek sponsorship from an employer'.[27] However, obtaining employer sponsorship was not a realistic possibility in most cases, as will be explained below.

---

26   Department of Immigration and Citizenship, *Processing of Priority Group 5 General Skilled Migration Applications*. Available at: www.immi.gov.au/skilled/general-skilled-migration/gsm-priority5-processing.htm (site discontinued).
27   Chris Evans, Minister for Immigration and Citizenship, 'Options Remain for Overseas Students' (Media Release, 9 February 2010).

As at 30 September 2013, there were still 11,380 PG5 people in Australia in the GSM pipeline.[28] The total number of applications in the GSM pipeline as at 30 September 2013 was 67,219 persons.[29] Meanwhile, the planning level (government quota) for the 2013–14 year for the GSM program was 73,840 — with new SkillSelect applicants being prioritised above all other categories.

As at 4 October 2013, applications from applicants in PG5 who had applied for the Skilled Independent visa (subclass 885) before 28 June 2010 were being allocated to a case officer for processing. For some of the provisional skilled visa classes, allocation had not commenced at all.[30]

This allocation date means that those applicants will have waited more than three years before their application is even allocated for processing. Given that one cannot apply until after completing one's Australian award, after a minimum of two years study, this means that these people have been living in Australia for a minimum of five years on temporary visas. Very many will have been living in Australia for even longer, depending on the number and type of courses they have undertaken — e.g. foundation studies and/or English language course (six months); bachelor degree course (three years); masters course (two years or more); PhD (three or four years or more). So, there will be some applicants in this group for whom Australia has effectively been home for the past 10 years, yet who are still existing in the limbo of temporary migration status — with all the detriment that that brings.

PG5 former students are languishing in an indeterminate pipeline of visa applicants. They remain as temporary residents, mostly not holding a substantive temporary visa but only a bridging visa. Their status, even as permanent visa applicants with a lawful right to remain in Australia, is precarious.[31] They are prevented from settling and formally becoming part of the Australian community — perpetual

---

28   Figures supplied by email from the Department of Immigration and Border Protection to the author, 21 October 2013.

29   Ibid.

30   Department of Immigration and Citizenship, *Allocation Dates for General Skilled Migration Applications*. Available at: www.immi.gov.au/skilled/general-skilled-migration/estimated-allocation-times.htm (site discontinued).

31   Note, for instance, the Migration Amendment (Visa Capping) Bill 2010 (Cth) (discussed above) sought to cancel a large number of GSM visa applications including from onshore applicants.

temporary residents, even though Australia has been their home for many years. They work, pay taxes, have Australian friends and relatives, and, in some cases, Australian-born children. Yet their lives are forced to be lived in a holding pattern.

As bridging visa holders, they are not prohibited from working, however, their temporary and precarious immigration status makes them unattractive to employers, at least for employment in professional and other skilled occupations. This forces them into semi-skilled or unskilled, low-paid work in which they are vulnerable to exploitation.[32] The longer they are not engaged in using their qualifications and knowledge, the more they are deskilling and going backwards. This personal reality is described by a member of PG5:

> In April 2008 I applied for the permanent residency (as a professional translator, supported by my law degree) with an expectation that I'd have a PR in 10 months (as my lawyer told me). Late of 2008, I was invited to take medical check and police record check by a case officer. After submitting all the required documents, I have been waiting for more than 2 years and … no one has touched my application since then. Altogether I've been waiting for 3 years and 5 months (til now).

> I'm not lucky as some of you guys who have found proper jobs. Except for 1 year working for the Uni while studying there, for 5 years I've worked for a supermarket. Not so bad job though but I worry that all knowledge and training I had achieved in studying are eventually dulling, day by day, in my manual work.[33]

---

32   See, for example, Fair Work Ombudsman, 'Convenience Store Operators Fined $150,000 for Underpaying International Students' (Media Release, 27 April 2011); Fair Work Ombudsman, 'Brisbane Café Back-Pays Students $120,000 after Fair Work Ombudsman Investigation' (Media Release, 22 February 2010); Victorian TAFE International and United Voice, 'Taken to the Cleaners: Experiences of International Students Working in the Australian Retail Cleaning Industry' (November 2012). Available at: hdl.voced.edu.au/10707/232836.

33   Mr G Nuyen posted this statement on a website created by G5rs: G4 online. Available at: www.g4online.org/About-Australian-Skilled-Migration-Group-5, accessed 3 May 2013. (Note that this website has since become inaccessible and original information is no longer available at this site, but see related sites at www.facebook.com/pages/Australian-GSM-Group-5-Applicants-Website/146625305386625 and www.facebook.com/pages/Australian-General-Skilled-Migration-Group-5previous-4/189378114433646.)

Many have incurred massive debts back home (and/or family have sold property to pay for their education in Australia) so there is a strong imperative for them to earn enough not just to pay for their living expenses in Australia but also to remit repayments on the outstanding loans.

As bridging visa holders, they do not have freedom to come and go from Australia. To obtain a bridging visa B, which allows re-entry, one needs to demonstrate substantial reasons for needing to leave. It also costs money to apply.

> Even now after 3 years of constant anticipation waiting to get what I (and all of us) rightfully deserve, my life is stagnant and all my goals and my personal growth are at a halt due to these policies. Employers continue to favour applicants with residency so nothing better works out, I cannot start my own business, cannot study and cannot go back to see my family without taking permission (which costs me again every time, and that too for no greater than 3 months under certain circumstances).[34]

There are other consequences of this group's temporary status: they are ineligible to sponsor their family members to join them in Australia. In some cases, partners are kept separated and children overseas remain separated from their parents in Australia. They are required to pay full fees for their children's schooling in Australia. They experience difficulty obtaining credit, including phone plans. As temporary or bridging visa holders, they are not eligible for social security support.

Former students affected by government policy reversals have limited options for normalising their status and their lives. Potential pathways are strewn with sometimes insurmountable hurdles. For instance, while they can try to find an Australian employer willing to sponsor them for an employer-sponsored permanent visa (RSMS or ENS), they are competing against other graduates, including Australian citizens and Australian permanent residents. The rules for eligibility for these visas require that the employer offers a three-year contract — which makes foreign graduates less attractive to employers. Visa eligibility criteria require a specified minimum salary to be offered, and require skilled work experience — which many overseas students will not have had

---

34   Ibid., Mr Tarun Kanda.

the chance to obtain. Similar obstacles pertain when attempting to find an Australian employer willing to sponsor them for a temporary employer-sponsored visa (with a pathway after three years to being sponsored for permanent residence). Some former students may resort to so-called 'visa-churning' — the series of visa applications that former students might go through in order to stay on lawfully[35] — while some may decide to risk staying in Australia unlawfully. Others may attempt legal action against the government to force the issue.[36] And, of course, some may return home, having 'failed' in Australia. For many former students, this would be a very difficult choice. Many have lived, worked, and strived to make a life for themselves in Australia over many years, and returning home would require them to begin again from scratch. It can involve loss of face for themselves and their families, and an ongoing burden of debt as repaying education-related loans will be much harder, if not impossible.

> I have spent 5 valuable years of my life in Australia and there has never been a day that I regret to date. However, if I am unable to remain in Australia permanently I will find it devastating for my son's development and for me and my husband's future as 5 years is a long time to be away from my country and to go back and rebuild our lives from scratch is beyond my frame of thinking let alone having to do same.[37]

Conclusion

When Chris Evans introduced priority processing, the minister said that the old system was 'just like pulling a ticket number from the dispenser at the supermarket deli counter' and waiting to be served.[38] He explained that it 'doesn't make sense' that Australia was 'taking hairdressers from overseas in front of doctors and nurses'.[39] As one commentator has pointed out, while this may be true from a national interest perspective, priority processing lacks procedural fairness

---

35   See Bob Birrell and Earnest Healy, 'Immigration Overshoot' (CPUR Research Report, Centre for Population and Urban Research, Monash University, 2012).

36   Bernard Lane, 'Irate Students May Not Go Home, Lawyer David Bitel Warns', *The Australian*, 24 September 2010. Available at: www.theaustralian.com.au/national-affairs/irate-students-may-not-go-home-lawyer-david-bitel-warns/story-fn59niix-1225928627942.

37   Nat, above fn 33.

38   Evans, above fn 16.

39   Ibid.

and has had devastating impacts for individual applicants.[40] Yet the personal detriment is also going to be felt at the national level. The inordinate delays in processing valid visa applications and granting visas has damaged these applicants' prospects for successful settlement and their ability to contribute to Australia to their full potential. The systematic delaying of settlement hindering the progression of people's lives and careers and the seemingly perpetual deferring of accepting this significant group of committed migrants formally into the community may be harmful not just to the individuals concerned but also to Australia's economic and social interests.

It is possible to make comparisons with temporary guest worker schemes, where 'the legal distinction between the status of citizen and of foreigner' will provide a clear criterion for conferring them with different political and social rights. But with the passage of time come 'inexorable pressures for settlement and community formation'.[41] However, there is a distinction: temporary worker schemes are devised on the basis that the stay will be limited and/or revocable, while in the case of the former international students in Australia, they were given the expectation that their stay as a temporary student could potentially be converted into permanent residence. Instead, they find themselves resident in Australia without the formal recognition of resident status.

Some within this group of people living in the twilight zone have tried to organise, to agitate, to explore legal action, to try to get public attention to put pressure on the government. These are the self-named 'G5rs'.[42] They are asserting their right to a conclusion to this process, which will allow them access to the rights of membership of this community they have been a part of and been contributing to for many years. But overall, they are a relatively small and hidden group whose plight goes unnoticed.

---

40   Peter Mares, 'Internationalisation and a Big Australia: Debates on Migration, Education and Population' (presentation at the TAFE Directors Australia 2011 National Conference, Sydney, 6 September 2011). Available at: www.tda.edu.au/cb_pages/files/TDA%20Internationalisation%20 and%20big%20Australia%20Mares%20060911%20RPL.pdf.
41   Peter Mares, 'International Students and the Law of Unintended Consequences', *Inside Story*, 28 September 2001, quoting Stephen Castles and Mark J Miller, *The Age of Migration: International Population Movements in the Modern World* (Palgrave Macmillan, 4th edition, 2009). Available at: inside.org.au/international-students-and-the-law-of-unintended-consequences/.
42   Website cited at fn 33.

It remains to be seen what policy-makers have learned from the experience of the G5rs. Certainly, students coming to Australia now are under no illusion that they will be eligible for permanent residence when they finish their course. The post-study work rights visa[43] that commenced in March 2013 was introduced to help the education industry to recover from the effects of the de-coupling of the student visa and skilled migration programs. But what further problems will this visa create? What will become of these former students at the end of the work visa period? Are we creating more permanent temporary migrants, with no confirmed pathway to permanent resident status?

In a speech in late 2013, the Minister for Education in the Coalition Government, Christopher Pyne, made comments in relation to post-study work rights: 'Our government will also give priority to reviewing post-study work rights to bring about clearer and more appropriate rules that maximise opportunities for graduates to convert world-leading qualifications to meaningful, needed careers.'[44]

Further comments by the minister indicate that the government is considering re-establishing a pathway from student status to permanent residence:

> This government will also seek to reverse the broad public perception which emerged under Labor that somehow foreign students must be prevented from getting a student visa on the basis they might one day aspire to live permanently in our great country.
>
> … But other students, those that study here, gain an Australian qualification, make friends, bring their family out to visit, participate in, and are able to contribute to our society by filling an area of genuine workforce shortage. They are exactly the kind of people we want, and should want, at the front of our migration list — not at the end.[45]

This raises the immediate question of how the government intends to treat the former students languishing in PG5 — people who appear to fit that exact description.

---

43   The Temporary Graduate Visa, subclass 485, allows those graduating with a bachelor degree and above to stay and work in Australia for a period up to four years (depending on the level of qualification).
44   Pyne, Christopher, 'A New Architecture for International Education' (speech at the Australian International Education Conference, Canberra, 9 October 2013) 8.
45   Ibid., 9.

In the context of swinging policies, each seemingly designed to ameliorate the unintended consequences of the previous, we can see the individuals detrimentally affected by the reversals as collateral damage. The rhetoric of blame shifting and the apparent reluctance with which the government has acted to rectify their position (by promptly processing their valid visa applications) indicates that while such individual harm was not intended, it is nevertheless an expedient consequence of the policies.

The final words go to one of the G5rs expressing the personal frustration felt by thousands of former international students whose legitimate expectations and need to formally participate in the Australian community were sacrificed in pursuit of a perceived national economic interest:

> We now form a committed, educated, reforming, restructuring and tax paying part of the Australian Population and Australian Economy. Yet we are denied the basic rights every other resident and citizen has.

> In conclusion to my story, I only plead to the DIAC [Department of Immigration and Citizenship] to have a fair go policy on us G5 applicants. We have been separated from our families, we have been diverted from our goals and our lives have been kept in Limbo for way too long now. Please consider the Values of Human *Rights and Respect for Human Life which is the PROUD EMBLEM OF AUSTRALIA.*[46]

Bibliography

Articles, books, and reports

Baas, Michiel, 'Students of Migration: Indian Overseas Students and the Question of Permanent Residency' (2006) 14 *People and Place* 8

Baas, Michiel, 'The Language of Migration: The Education Industry Versus the Migration Industry' (2007) 15 *People and Place* 49

Birrell, Bob and Ernest Healy, 'The February 2010 Reforms and the International Student Industry' (2010) 18 *People and Place* 65

---

46   Mr Tarun Kanda, above fn 33 and 34.

Birrell, Bob and Earnest Healy, 'Immigration Overshoot' (CPUR Research Report, Centre for Population and Urban Research, Monash University, 2012)

Birrell, Bob and Bronwen Perry, 'Immigration Policy Change and the International Student Industry' (2009) 17 *People and Place* 64

Castles, Stephen and Mark J Miller, *The Age of Migration: International Population Movements in the Modern World* (Palgrave Macmillan, 4th edition, 2009)

Crock, Mary and Laurie Berg, *Immigration Refugees and Forced Migration: Law, Policy and Practice in Australia* (The Federation Press, 2011)

Davis, Dorothy and Bruce Mackintosh (eds), *Making a Difference: Australian International Education* (UNSW Press, 2011)

Hawthorne, Lesleyanne, 'Designer Immigrants? International Students and Two-Step Migration' in Darla K Deardorff et al. (eds), *The SAGE Handbook of International Higher Education* (SAGE Publications, 2012)

Knight, Michael, 'Strategic Review of the Student Visa Program 2011' (Report to the Australian Government, June 2011). Available at: www.border.gov.au/ReportsandPublications/Documents/reviews-and-inquiries/2011-knight-review.pdf

McCarthy, John et al., 'Perceptions Taskforce Beyond the Lost Decade' (Report of the Australia India Institute, 2012)

Meadows, Eric, 'From Aid to Industry: A History of International Education in Australia' in Dorothy Davis and Bruce Mackintosh (eds), *Making a Difference: Australian International Education* (UNSW Press, 2011)

Sing, Supriya and Anuja Cabraal, 'Indian Student Migrants in Australia: Issues of Community Sustainability' (2010) 18 *People and Place* 19

Ziguras, Christopher and Siew-Fang Law, 'Recruiting International Students as Skilled Migrants: The Global "Skills Race" as Viewed from Australia and Malaysia' (2006) 4 *Globalisation, Societies and Education* 59

Legislation

Migration Amendment (Visa Capping) Bill 2010 (Cth)

Migration Regulations 1994 (Cth)

Other

Australian Bureau of Statistics, 'Australian Social Trends December 2011: International Students'. Available at: www.abs.gov.au/ AUSSTATS/abs@.nsf/allprimarymainfeatures/573AD76DFABE2D FCCA2579CE000BAD25?opendocument

Australian Education International, *International Student Data*. Available at: internationaleducation.gov.au/research/International-Student-Data/Pages/default.aspx

Australian Education International, 'Research Snapshot, Export Income to Australia from Education Services in 2009' (2010) . Available at: www.aei.gov.au/research/Research-Snapshots/Documents/Export %20Income%202009-10.pdf (site discontinued)

Council of Australian Governments, 'International Students Strategy for Australia 2010–2014'. Available at: www.coag.gov.au/sites/default/ files/International%20Students%20Strategy%20-%20PDF.pdf

Dai, Louis, David Elliot-Jones and Lachlan McLeod, *Convenient Education* (Chocolate Liberation Front, 2012)

Department of Immigration and Citizenship, *Allocation Dates for General Skilled Migration Applications*. Available at: www.immi. gov.au/skilled/general-skilled-migration/estimated-allocation-times.htm (site discontinued)

Department of Immigration and Citizenship, *Fact Sheet 24a: Priority Processing for Skilled Migration Visas* (July 2012). Available at: www.immi.gov.au/media/fact-sheets/24apriority_skilled.htm (site discontinued)

Department of Immigration and Citizenship, *Processing of Priority Group 5 General Skilled Migration Applications*. Available at: www. immi.gov.au/skilled/general-skilled-migration/gsm-priority5-processing.htm (site discontinued)

Evans, Chris, Minister for Immigration and Citizenship, 'Changes to Australia's Skilled Migration Program' (Speech delivered at The Australian National University, Canberra, 8 February 2010)

Evans, Chris, Minister for Immigration and Citizenship, 'Migration Reforms to Deliver Australia's Skills Needs' (Media Release, 8 February 2010)

Evans, Chris, Minister for Immigration and Citizenship, 'Options Remain for Overseas Students' (Media Release, 9 February 2010)

Evans, Chris, Minister for Immigration and Citizenship, 'New Skilled Occupation List to Meet Australia's Economic Needs' (Media Release, 17 May 2010)

Evans, Chris, Minister for Immigration and Citizenship, 'Migration Options Remain for Chefs and Cooks' (Media Release, 18 May 2010)

Evans, Chris, Minister for Immigration and Citizenship, 'International Students Welcome in Australia' (Media Release, 10 June 2010)

Evans, Chris, Minister for Immigration and Citizenship, 'Australia Continues to Welcome International Students' (Media Release, 8 September 2010)

Fair Work Ombudsman, 'Brisbane Café Back-Pays Students $120,000 after Fair Work Ombudsman Investigation' (Media Release, 22 February 2010)

Fair Work Ombudsman, 'Convenience Store Operators Fined $150,000 for Underpaying International Students' (Media Release, 27 April 2011)

G4 online. Available at: www.g4online.org/About-Australian-Skilled-Migration-Group-5, accessed 3 May 2013. (Note that this website has since become inaccessible and original information is no longer available at this site, but see related sites at www.facebook.com/pages/Australian-GSM-Group-5-Applicants-Website/146625305386625 and www.facebook.com/pages/Australian-General-Skilled-Migration-Group-5previous-4/189378114433646)

Jensen, Erik, 'Some Private Colleges Are Visa Factories', *The Sydney Morning Herald,* 28 March 2007. Available at www.smh.com.au/news/national/some-private-colleges-are-visa-factories-study/2007/03/27/1174761471743.html

Koleth, Elsa, 'Overseas Students: Immigration Policy Changes 1997–May 2010' (Background Note, Parliamentary Library, 18 June 2010)

Lane, Bernard, 'Irate Students May Not Go Home, Lawyer David Bitel Warns', *The Australian*, 24 September 2010. Available at: www.theaustralian.com.au/national-affairs/irate-students-may-not-go-home-lawyer-david-bitel-warns/story-fn59niix-1225928627942

Mares, Peter, 'International Students and the Law of Unintended Consequences', *Inside Story*, 28 September 2001. Available at: inside.org.au/international-students-and-the-law-of-unintended-consequences/

Mares, Peter, 'Internationalisation and a Big Australia: Debates on Migration, Education and Population' (presentation at the TAFE Directors Australia 2011 National Conference, Sydney, 6 September 2011). Available at: www.tda.edu.au/cb_pages/files/TDA%20Internationalisation%20and%20big%20Australia%20Mares%20060911%20RPL.pdf

Mares, Peter, 'Temporary Migration Is a Permanent Thing', *Inside Story*, 20 March 2013. Available at: inside.org.au/temporary-migration-is-a-permanent-thing/

O'Malley, Nick, 'Visa Racket Leaves Foreign Students Exposed', *The Sydney Morning Herald*, 16 July 2009. Available at: www.smh.com.au/national/visa-racket-leaves-foreign-students-exposed-20090715-dlja.html

Pyne, Christopher, 'A New Architecture for International Education' (Speech at the Australian International Education Conference, Canberra, 9 October 2013)

Trounson, Andrew, 'Humanity Denied in a Dash for Cash', *The Australian*, 5 May 2010. Available at: www.theaustralian.com.au/higher-education/humanity-denied-in-a-dash-for-cash/story-e6frgcjx-1225862224911

Victorian TAFE International and United Voice, 'Taken to the Cleaners: Experiences of International Students Working in the Australian Retail Cleaning Industry' (November 2012). Available at: hdl.voced.edu.au/10707/232836

Web archive, *Study in Australia Website*. Available at: web.archive.org/web/20070620161512/www.studyinaustralia.gov.au/Sia/en/AfterYourStudies/Employment

3

Intertwined Mobilities of Education, Tourism and Labour: The Consequences of 417 and 485 Visas in Australia

Shanthi Robertson

Abstract[1]

This chapter focuses on some of the consequences of recent expansions to skilled temporary graduate (subclass 485) and working holiday (subclass 417) visa programs in Australia. These visa categories allow for extended periods of work and residence, primarily among young people who are seeking an overseas work/life experience or a pathway to more permanent migration. Using data from a pilot study into the life and work experiences of 485 and 417 workers in Australia, the chapter explores the complex and heterogeneous kinds of migrant subjectivities and trajectories created by these visa schemes, and the intersections of labour, education, and tourism policies in which they are embedded. It addresses the kinds of labour market experiences that result from these intersections, and also explores the

---

1   Sections of the introductory material in this chapter were originally published in Shanthi Robertson (2014) 'Time and Temporary Migration: The Case of Temporary Graduate Workers and Working Holiday Makers in Australia' (2014) 40(12) *Journal of Ethnic and Migration Studies*: 1915–1933, reprinted by permission of Taylor & Francis Ltd, www.tandfonline.com.

consequences of these migration pathways to understandings of social relations and belonging. Finally, it argues that neoliberalised systems of immigration governance intersect with the intentions, desires, and social practices of 485 and 417 workers to produce two main effects. First, significant flows of precarious foreign workers into diverse segments of the labour market are effectively hidden from public view. Second, complex migration trajectories and identities are constructed within which the boundaries between skilled/unskilled, legal/illegal, and temporary/permanent become increasingly blurred. These effects serve specific political and economic agendas yet also have broader and often unintended impacts on migration as a process of social transformation in Australia.

Introduction

Temporariness and circularity are increasingly important dimensions of migration processes on a global scale, with the boundaries around categories of temporary mobility and permanent mobility becoming increasingly blurry.[2] Traditional models of one-way mobility, settlement, and integration are giving way to understandings of the transnationality and temporariness of diverse migrant subjects, from elite knowledge workers to unskilled contract labour, with implications for the governance of migration as well as for new forms of migrant agency.[3] These global trends are very much apparent in Australia where a settler society identity, built up since the beginnings of post-war mass immigration, is being transformed by significant recent increases to temporary migration schemes.

The focus is on the consequences, both intended and unintended, of two specific temporary visa categories: the Temporary Graduate (subclass 485) and Working Holiday (subclass 417) visas. Recent policy changes to these visa categories allow for extended periods of work and residence in Australia, primarily among young people who

---

2   Stephen Castles, 'Migration and Community Formation under Conditions of Globalization' (2002) 36 *International Migration Review* 1143.
3   A M Findlay, 'From Settlers to Skilled Transients: The Changing Structure of British International Migration' (1988) 19(4) *Geoforum* 401; Patricia Landolt and Lurin Goldring, 'Caught in the Work–Citizenship Matrix: The Lasting Effects of Precarious Legal Status on Work for Toronto Immigrants' (2011) 8 *Globalizations* 325; Aihwa Ong, 'Mutations in Citizenship' (2006) 23(2–3) *Theory, Culture and Society* 499.

are seeking an overseas work/life experience or a pathway to more permanent migration. More than just 'sojourners', 485 workers and 417 workers may live and work in Australia without a permanent status for between one and four years on these specific visas. Durations are often even longer as transitioning through other temporary visa categories (visa 'churn') is common.[4] While under-researched and politically 'hidden' by their associations with education and tourism rather than labour migration,[5] these schemes are creating diverse flows of migrants who disturb the boundaries around identities of tourist, student, worker and the dualities of skilled/unskilled, legal/ illegal, and temporary/permanent.[6] Allon, Anderson and Bushell aptly describe these types of flows as 'mutant mobilities', that is, they are made up of mobile subjects that have multiple and heterogeneous goals and intentions surrounding their mobility.[7]

Furthering qualitative understandings of the experiences of these migrant workers is important. Evidence suggests that migrant agency is reshaping Australian temporary visa categories in various ways[8] and ignoring the role of human agency in the analysis of migration governance, particularly temporary migration schemes, often leads to a failure to meet stated policy objectives and unintended social and political consequences.[9] This is particularly significant research in the

---

4   Bob Birrell and Earnest Healy, 'Immigration Overshoot' (CPUR Research Report, Centre for Population and Urban Research, Monash University, 2012).

5   Ibid.

6   Fiona Allon and Kay Anderson, 'Intimate Encounters: The Embodied Transnationalism of Backpackers and Independent Travellers' (2010) 16 *Population, Space and Place* 11; Peter Mares, 'Temporary Migration and Its Implications for Australia' (speech to the Australian Senate, 23 September 2011). Available at: www.aph.gov.au/About_Parliament/Senate/Powers_practice_n_procedures/~/media/FB57E1420B9748698CCB4B84A799F08D.ashx; Shanthi Robertson, *Transnational Student-Migrants and the State: The Education-Migration Nexus* (Palgrave Macmillan, 2013).

7   Fiona Allon, Kay Anderson and Robyn Bushell, 'Mutant Mobilities: Backpacker Tourism in "Global" Sydney' (2008) 3 *Mobilities* 73.

8   Robert Guthrie, 'Tourists Overstaying Their Welcome: When the Visa Runs Out and the Workers Stay On' (2004) 6 *The Tourism Industry* 22; Haeyoung Jang, Kyungja Jung and Bronwen Dalton, 'Factors Influencing Labour Migration of Korean Women into the Entertainment and Sex Industry in Australia' (Paper presented at 6th Biennial Korean Studies Association of Australasia, University of Sydney, 8–9 July 2009); Peter Mares, above fn 6; Shanthi Robertson, 'Cash Cows, Backdoor Migrants, or Activist Citizens? International Students, Citizenship, and Rights in Australia' (2011) 34 *Ethnic and Racial Studies* 2192.

9   Stephen Castles, 'The Factors That Make and Unmake Migration Policies' (2004) 38 *International Migration Review* 852; Martin Ruhs, 'The Potential of Temporary Migration Programmes in Future International Migration Policy' (2006) 145(1–2) *International Labour Review* 7.

Australian context because norms around migration are arguably still embedded within a 'settler-citizen' paradigm, and understandings of temporary migrant experiences are particularly limited.

This chapter discusses some findings from the pilot stage of an ongoing project that seeks to understand what 'being temporary' means to these diverse flows of migrant workers now living and working in Australia — what it means to social relations, to labour experiences, and to the spatio-temporal reordering of migrant journeys. In-depth interviews with 20 participants from a range of source countries who hold or have held a 485 or 417 visa while residing in Australia were conducted, as well as four interviews with representatives from non-government organisations who work specifically with these migrants. Because the policy-based designations of 'skilled temporary graduate' and 'working holiday maker' often do not match with the intentions, identities or labour market participation of the migrants themselves, they are referred to as '485 workers' and '417 workers' respectively.

The focus here is on the consequences of these visa policies, for individual migrants' work and social experiences, and for broader transformations of Australian immigration paradigms. In particular, this chapter addresses how these particular visa regimes are crafting specific kinds of migrant journeys and vulnerabilities. I commence with a brief policy overview of the two schemes, particularly focusing on recent changes, and then concentrating on how these visa policies structure complex intersections between labour, tourism, and education in migrants' journeys, with policy and status constraints often transforming engagements with work and study in various ways. I then analyse the labour market experiences of 417 and 485 workers, revealing how, despite the diverse kinds of work that they do, temporary status makes these migrants inherently vulnerable as workers in a number of ways. Finally, I look to the social dimensions of 485 and 417 worker pathways, analysing the ways in which constructions of temporariness structure how these groups are positioned in terms of the settled ethnic communities that they have links to, and in terms of the broader Australian public. I conclude with a summative analysis of the broad consequences of 417 and 485 worker schemes. This highlights the specific economic and labour market consequences as largely intended, and serving particular political and economic agendas, but also notes the unintended social and political consequences that occur through the transformation of settler-citizen migration paradigms. While this chapter focuses qualitatively on the social and work experiences of temporary migrants, in the following chapter, Peter Mares further expands understandings of the unintended consequences of temporary migration by pointing specifically to case studies in which legal and social rights and entitlements are contested, addressing broader questions around political belonging.

Methods

This chapter draws on a pilot study consisting of 20 semi-structured interviews with 417 workers (10 interviews) and 485 workers (10 interviews) from South Korea, Taiwan, the United Kingdom, Ireland, Sweden, China, Iran and the Netherlands. The intent was to build as diverse a sample as possible, with snowball sampling used to recruit participants after initial contacts were made. It also draws on four interviews with key informants from three non-government organisations that worked closely with 417 and 485 workers on workplace and immigration issues.

Migrant participants were asked about their plans, decisions, expectations, and intentions around their mobility, and their work and social experiences while in Australia. Key informants were asked about the general experiences of the migrants on these visas that they work with, particularly the issues they face in the workplace and issues of belonging and social relations. Interviews were approximately one hour in length, and were tape recorded and transcribed. Pseudonyms are used for all participants throughout the analysis. This methodology is based on the arguments for using migrant stories as a means to understand how their agency shapes and is shaped by migration governance and dominant discourses around migration. While not providing a comprehensive or representative analysis of 417 and 485 worker experiences, these methods provide an exploratory analysis of an under-researched group of migrants and the consequences of recent policy change — an analysis that points to several avenues for future research.

Policy context and recent developments

Working holiday schemes have a long history in Australia, having been initially introduced in 1975, while temporary graduate schemes were first introduced in 2007 and substantially expanded at the beginning of 2013. However, both categories are increasing in significance in terms of both the number of visas granted and the extent of work rights attached to them (which will be discussed below). Annual 485 visa grants more than doubled between 2009 and 2012,[10] while the 417 program grew about 23 per cent between 2011 and 2012, with generally steady growth over the last decade.[11] The types of migration trajectories that they engender, and the types of migrants they attract, also have a number of similarities.[12] There are, however, key differences in the work rights and eligibility criteria for these visas. This section will briefly outline the key policies around the two schemes.

Working holiday schemes are reciprocal agreements between Australia and select countries that allow young people to live and work in Australia on a temporary basis. Currently, the working holiday program encompasses two visas, the Working Holiday Visa (subclass 417) and the Work and Holiday Visa (subclass 462), which apply to passport holders of different countries. The majority of working holiday makers enter Australia under the 417 subclass, which is the focus of this chapter. The top 12 source countries for the 417 visa are the UK, South Korea, Germany, Ireland, France, Taiwan, Canada, Japan, Italy, Sweden, Hong Kong, and the Netherlands.

Basic eligibility requirements for working holiday visas state that applicants must be aged 18–30 at the time of applying; not be accompanied by dependent children during their stay in Australia; meet health, character, and financial requirements; and have a sufficient amount of funds for a return ticket or an actual return ticket.

---

10   Peter Mares, 'Graduate Visas May Yet Prove Controversial' *The Age*, 4 April 2013. Available at: www.theage.com.au/comment/graduate-visas-may-yet-prove-controversial-20130403-2h706. html#ixzz314WqNveK.

11   Department of Immigration and Citizenship, 'Record Interest in Australia's Visitor Visa Programs' (2013). Available at: migrationblog.border.gov.au/2013/03/01/record-interest-in-australias-visitor-visa-programs/.

12   Shanthi Robertson, 'Time and Temporary Migration: The Case of Temporary Graduate Workers and Working Holiday Makers in Australia' (2014) 40(12) *Journal of Ethnic and Migration Studies*.

Initially, working holiday visas were valid for stays of 12 months only and, although there were no limitations on the type of employment, 417 workers could only spend a maximum of three months working for any single employer. From July 2006, however, the maximum time spent with a single employer increased from three to six months, and holders of a 417 visa became able to apply for a second 12-month visa if they spent 88 consecutive days during their first visa doing 'specified work' in regional Australia.

'Specified work' includes work in plant and animal cultivation, fishing and pearling, or mining and construction. 'Regional Australia' encompasses a broad geographic space, including capital cities and suburban areas in some states.[13]

Most 417 workers seeking the one-year extension (bringing their total time in Australia as a 417 worker to two years) spend their 88 days doing unskilled seasonal agricultural work, such as fruit picking.[14] However, skilled tradespeople on working holiday visas also work in regional construction and mining industries. The 417 workers who receive a second visa are then free to pursue any employment of their choice during their second year, although they are again limited to spending a maximum of six months with any one employer. The 417 workers are also free to study for up to four months per year. More than 220,000 working holiday maker visas were granted in 2011–12, and at the end of 2012 there were more than 162,000 working holiday makers residing in Australia.[15]

The Skilled–Graduate (subclass 485) visa was initially introduced in 2007 as an 18-month temporary work visa for eligible international graduates of Australian universities. It was superseded by the Temporary Graduate (subclass 485) visa in early 2013, which provided considerably expanded time frames. As of early 2013, international

---

13   The whole of the states of Tasmania, South Australia, and the Northern Territory, including their cities, are classed as 'regional Australia' under the working holiday visa requirements for second visas. In other states, only major cities/urban centres and surrounding areas are excluded under the classification of 'regional Australia', with the exception of the Australian Capital Territory, which is excluded in its entirety. In New South Wales, 'regional Australia' excludes Sydney, Newcastle, the Central Coast, and Wollongong; in Western Australia it excludes Perth and surrounding areas; and in Victoria the Melbourne metropolitan area is excluded.

14   Yan Tan and Laurence Hester, 'Labour Market and Economic Impacts of International Working Holiday Temporary Migrants to Australia' (2011) 18 *Population, Space and Place* 359.

15   Department of Immigration and Citizenship, above fn 11.

students in Australia who obtained their first student visa after November 2011, and who have completed at minimum a bachelor's degree involving at least two years study in Australia, are eligible for a post-study work visa of between two and four years, depending on their level of qualification.

The 2013 changes to the 485 visa category are the most recent iteration of a series of policies in Australia, beginning in the late 1990s, that linked international education to skilled migration. Initially, these policies provided specific pathways for international students to become permanent residents. This proved to be controversial, and the subsequent Knight Review of the Student Visa Program limited direct pathways from study to permanence while liberalising access to and duration of temporary graduate visas. International students with Australian bachelor's or master's by coursework degrees are eligible for a two-year temporary post-study work visa. Master's by research graduates are eligible for three years and PhD graduates for four. Graduates do not require employer sponsorship or specific skills to qualify for this visa, and there are no limitations on rights to work or study.

There were over 38,000 skilled graduate visa holders in Australia at the end of 2012, an increase of 74 per cent on 2011 figures.[16] Yet the liberalisation of access to graduate visas from early 2013 means these numbers are likely to increase considerably over the next few years, especially given the popularity of previous post-study work schemes in Australia and in other countries. The vast majority of migrants currently under the 485 scheme are Chinese and Indian, reflecting the international student population.

---

16   Department of Immigration and Citizenship, *Temporary Entrants and New Zealand Citizens in Australia* (2012). Available at: www.border.gov.au/ReportsandPublications/Documents/statistics/temp-entrants-newzealand-dec12.pdf.

Intertwined mobilities: Complex engagements with work, study, and leisure travel

The temporary graduate and working holiday schemes are the only temporary work visas in Australia that do not require direct employer sponsorship or a specific skill set, meaning that 417 and 485 workers differ in a number of crucial ways from other streams of migrant labour. They sit in a strange policy space, both apart from the highly selective permanent skilled migration program, and apart from sponsored skilled temporary visas, such as the 457, which require migrants to be sponsored by an employer and often require some level of labour market testing.

Politically, and often in the public imagination, 485 and 417 workers are still connected to processes seen to be separate from 'genuine' labour migration — that is, international education and tourism, respectively. In fact, to a large extent, 485 and 417 workers are scarcely acknowledged as migrant workers at all, connected instead to transient and consumption-based identities of 'students' and 'backpackers'. Official information targeted towards potential 417 workers and the general public continues to position the visa as intended for 'cultural exchange', and to place the work component as secondary to the tourism component.[17]

Similarly, the Knight Review, as the key document framing the new 485 visa policy, insists that the visas are for temporary residence only, that they function as 'an adjunct to study', and should not be seen as pathways to permanent migration.[18] However, a key consequence of that policy has been an inseparable intertwining of mobilities of labour, education, and tourism. The labour component, in particular, is an increasingly important aspect of these visa programs. This has subsequently created porousness between temporalities of permanence

---

17   Department of Immigration and Citizenship, 'Working Holiday Maker Visa Program Report' (30 June 2013). Available at: www.border.gov.au/ReportsandPublications/Documents/statistics/ working-holiday-report-jun13.pdf.

18   Knight, Michael, 'Strategic Review of the Student Visa Program' (Report to the Australian Government, June 2011).

and temporariness, and created complex engagements with work, study, and leisure travel in the context of the varied and dynamic migration goals of the migrants themselves.

Despite the continued official rhetoric of encouraging tourism and cultural exchange, the Department of Immigration and Citizenship's[19] decision to extend the working holiday visa to two years and to include the regional work requirement indicates that the scheme is no longer primarily about facilitating an extended cultural and tourist experience for young travellers, but in fact it is about bringing specific forms of temporary labour into Australia.[20] Similarly, although positioned as an 'adjunct to study' in policy, 485 workers have full work rights for up to four years post-study, and previous research shows that post-study work visas are frequently used by migrants as a stepping stone to permanent residency.[21]

In gaining an in-depth understanding of the participants' journeys, one of the most significant themes is that 485 and 417 worker journeys involve complex goals around migration, study, work, and leisure. Work, however, is generally the central focus. The realities of the migration experience often see these goals unrealised or drastically transformed throughout the process. The 417 and 485 workers across the board tended to see their temporary visas either as a means to earn money and gain valuable professional experience before returning home or on-migrating to a third country, or as a stepping stone to a more permanent stay in Australia. While leisure travel was still a component of the experience for some, it usually came secondary to economic and long-term migration goals.

Most of the British and Irish 417 workers, for example, hoped that the initial visa would lead to employer sponsorship for a 457 or a permanent visa, seeing this pathway as a chance to escape from the high cost of living and limited work opportunities in cities such as London and Dublin. This further substantiates previous empirical research and media reports that point to increasing numbers of

---

19   The Department of Immigration and Citizenship (DIAC) changed its name in October 2013 to the Department of Immigration and Border Protection (DIBP). The majority of the fieldwork for this project occurred prior to the name change, the chapter thus refers to the department as DIAC throughout.

20   Bob Birrell and Earnest Healy, above fn 4.

21   Shanthi Robertson, above fn 6.

migrants using these visas primarily for the purposes of work rather than tourism,[22] especially in the context of ongoing recession or limited opportunities in key source countries. While 485 and 417 workers were generally keen to find professional employment, they also often needed to engage in whatever work they could find to pay off the debts accumulated by study, or to cover living costs and build savings for the future.[23]

While 'status mobility'[24] across different visa categories and intersecting study, work, and travel goals were common in all 417 and 485 workers' narratives, the trajectories varied considerably in different cases, and intentions and expectations around the purpose and duration of mobility frequently transformed over time. In speaking with representatives of organisations working with Taiwanese and Korean 417 workers, for example, I was told that the visa is often initially seen as a means to develop English language capabilities, gain foreign work experience, and save money to take back home. The working holiday period can also be a gateway to further study in Australia — a means to bolster English language skills so migrants eventually meet the requirements for tertiary study as international students, as well as to trial living in Australia before they commit to staying for a degree. Some leisure travel is often planned for the end of the stay, once significant funds have been saved by working.

Agents in the home countries convince potential 417 workers that after a few months of English language study they will be able to gain professional employment in Australia in well-paid jobs relating to their future career. However, this is seldom the reality. Most are unable to find professional work, and end up in unskilled work in co-ethnic-owned businesses. They often spend more money and time than they intended on language school when they discover their English skills are insufficient for the Australian labour market.

22   Luke O'Neill, '"Deep Recession" Cited in Irish Man's Visa Review', *Irish Echo*, 18 March 2011. Available at: www.irishecho.com.au/2011/03/18/deep-recession-cited-in-irish-mans-visa-review/8150; Ciara Kenney, 'Canada Doubles Quota of Irish Working Holiday Visas', *The Irish Times*, 6 October 2012. Available at: www.irishtimes.com/news/canada-doubles-quota-of-irish-working-holiday-visas-1.548331; Marie Madden, 'Galway's "Gathering" Down Under', *Galway Independent*, 13 March 2013; Bob Birrell and Earnest Healy, above fn 4.
23   Michiel Baas, *Imagined Mobility: Migration and Transnationalism Among Indian Students in Australia* (Anthem Press, 2010); Shanthi Robertson, above fn 6.
24   Liza Schuster, 'The Continuing Mobility of Migrants in Italy: Shifting Between Places and Statuses' (2005) 31 *Journal of Ethnic and Migration Studies* 757.

They are also often woefully misinformed about the cost of living in cities like Melbourne and Sydney and the average wages. As the end of the first year approaches, goals of saving, English competence, work experience and travel are unrealised. This prompts many to undertake the regional three months work to gain a second visa. After two years, many return home having spent the majority of their time in one place (with the exception of the regional three months), living with and working with other co-ethnic 417 workers in unskilled and poorly paid jobs.

The other highly significant consequence here is that migration policy itself, particular visa status and the criteria that have to be met to obtain extended stays or permanence, hinders meaningful engagement with study and work, and often forces migrants to renegotiate their goals in complex ways. One participant, Abdul, graduated with an engineering degree from a reputable Australian university. He found, however, once on his 485 visa, that he was unable to obtain a graduate position in his field, despite good marks and strong English. Government positions were available only to citizens, and the HR departments of engineering companies either explicitly or implicitly rejected him on the basis that he did not have permanent residency. Many of his fellow graduates on 485 visas were relegated to working in car washes or convenience stores to survive, and hoping for a better job to come along. Abdul, however, decided to change tack and return to study, and successfully gained a scholarship to do his PhD. The PhD, however, was really only a stop-gap solution to extend his time in Australia with a new student visa. Abdul was planning to apply for permanent residency and keep looking for jobs and sponsorship during his PhD candidature. If either came through, he would drop out of his PhD to join the workforce.

Liu, a Chinese graduate with a Master of Accounting, experienced a similar reconfiguration of work and study goals in the pursuit of a migration outcome. After graduation, Liu felt fortunate to obtain a job she enjoyed at a small accounting firm. However, she desperately needed to get a certain score on the International English Language Testing System (IELTS) exam for her permanent residence application to be successful. She had already failed to get the score she needed on previous tests. With the time on her temporary 485 visa running out,

Liu felt compelled to resign from her accounting job and take a casual hospitality job in the evenings, so that she would have her days free to devote to IELTS study.

Such negotiations of deskilling, reskilling, and changing pathways to buy more time in Australia or meet migration-driven outcomes are commonplace within the nexus of education, tourism, and labour. Temporary workers on a subclass 417 visa, for example, frequently leave skilled professional positions to complete the three-month regional work requirement. Ironically, Australian immigration governance discourses heavily place value on skilled workers. Yet the explicit and implicit limitations that 485 and 417 visas impose on migrants' agency in the labour force often means that workers with tertiary qualifications and professional experience end up in unskilled work.

Contemporary Australian migration processes in this context are increasingly complex, circular, and varied in terms of stages and durations.[25] The boundaries between permanent and temporary mobility are becoming increasingly porous and contingent, as some of these migrants engage in long and often protracted journeys to achieve extended stays and eventual permanence.[26] A key consequence of this is the creation of 'staggered pathways'[27] of temporal uncertainty that migrants must navigate to achieve their migration and life goals. Policy frameworks intimately impact on migrants' lives and choices, as visa conditions seek to govern migrants' time horizons and spatial location within particular regions and markets. While this spatial regulation is more explicit for 417 workers with the regional work requirements, it also impacts on many 485 workers because there are often more opportunities for employer sponsorship in regional areas through the Regional Sponsored Migration Scheme (RSMS).

The 485 and 417 workers also represent a 'middling experience'[28] of temporary labour migration, positioned somewhere between elite transnational knowledge workers and exploitable, unskilled migrant workers. They usually have a relatively high level of education, but

---

25   Graeme Hugo, 'In and Out of Australia' (2008) 4 *Asian Population Studies* 267.
26   Siew-Ean Khoo and Graeme Hugo, 'Which Skilled Temporary Migrants Become Permanent Residents and Why?' (2008) 42 *International Migration Review* 193; Shanthi Robertson, above fn 6.
27   Shanthi Robertson, above fn 6.
28   Brenda Yeoh, Katie Willis and Abdul Fakhri, 'Introduction: Transnationalism and Its Edges' (2003) 26(2) *Ethnic and Racial Studies* 207.

engage in both skilled and unskilled labour,[29] and in shadow labour economies.[30] They also represent a middling form of migration in the sense that, temporally, legally and socially, they sit somewhere between the 'sojourner' and the 'citizen'. While some will remain in Australia for a relatively short time, others face protracted journeys towards eventual permanent membership.

'Dodgy' jobs: Precariousness, semi-compliance and exploitation in the workplace

Although the 485 and 417 workers interviewed worked across a range of industries (including nursing, accounting, hospitality, community work, agriculture, administration, and marketing) and in a range of roles, precariousness and vulnerability in the workplace was the common thread in their stories. Nearly every migrant interviewed had experienced some kind of corrupt or illegal practice in the workplace. Some of these breaches were of benefit to the migrants — such as the falsification of hours or duties by employers so 417 visa holders could gain eligibility for a second visa — but most were exploitative in nature. The breaches of workplace laws and norms ranged from relatively mundane practices, such as workers paid cash-in-hand to avoid paying superannuation and penalty rates, to major breaches including verbal and sexual harassment, non-payment for hours worked, forcing workers to act as sub-contractors, and labour agencies or employers deducting exorbitant fees for placements, accommodation, or transport. As is often the case with temporary workers, employers tended to exploit the structural constraints imposed on temporary workers by their visa status,[31] and in particular their desires for permanent or extended stays.

---

29   Yan Tan and Laurence Hester, above fn 14.
30   Robert Guthrie, above fn 8; Haeyoung Jang, Kyungja Jung and Bronwen Dalton, above fn 8.
31   Selvaraj Velayutham, 'Precarious Experiences of Indians in Australia on 457 Temporary Work Visas' (2013) 24 *The Economic and Labour Relations Review* 340; Stefanie Toh and Michael Quinlan, 'Safeguarding the Global Contingent Workforce?: Guestworkers in Australia' (2009) 30 *International Journal of Manpower* 453.

Much of the 417 or 485 labour experiences fell into the realm of what Martin Ruhs and Bridget Anderson refer to as 'semi-compliance'.[32] In contrast to the false dichotomy between 'legal' and 'illegal' migration, Ruhs and Anderson use the term 'semi-compliance' to refer to employment practices whereby migrant workers are legally resident in the country, but are in some way in breach of the restrictions on their visa.[33] In the cases discussed here, however, 'semi-compliance' relates not just to the restrictions on the current visa, but also to employers and workers engaging in illegal practices to extend visas or obtain new visas. It can also encompass workplaces that provide some, but not all, of workers' legal wages and entitlements. The slang term 'dodgy' seemed to have been adopted by 417 and 485 workers of different cultures as a way to describe these employment situations of semi-compliance. Dodgy employers occupied an ambivalent place in the workers' imaginations — while on the one hand they could be exploitative, on the other hand, a dodgy workplace could be more inclined to support bypassing immigration requirements to the benefit of the worker.

Some of the worst stories of abuse in this study came from the regional work requirements for second 417 visas. For example, two British 417 visa holders were promised three months of agricultural work on a farming property so they could gain eligibility for a second visa. Once they arrived, they were instead tasked with providing 24-hour care for the family's six young children, and painting and decorating the family home, sometimes for up to 12 hours a day. They were not paid beyond the provision of room and board, which consisted of a shared room and bed (although the workers were not a couple) and the same dry cereal and plain cheese sandwiches for every meal. The impending expiry dates of their first visas and their concern that they would not find other regional work in time meant that they did not complain about the conditions or the lack of pay. In another instance, a Taiwanese 417 worker at a regional vegetable processing plant complained to her supervisor about underpayment and poor

---

32   Martin Ruhs and Bridget Anderson, 'Semi-Compliance and Illegality in Migrant Labour Markets: An Analysis of Migrants, Employers and the State in the UK' (2010) 16 *Population, Space and Place* 195.
33   Ibid.

safety conditions, and eventually threatened to take complaints to the Fair Work Ombudsman. She was subsequently harassed with threatening phone calls.

Work in urban centres, however, often also consisted of varying levels of exploitation. As discussed above, many large employers in Australia will not consider applicants with a temporary visa status, despite the fact that they have work rights.[34] As a result of this, 485 and 417 workers were often pushed into specific types of employment, usually highly casualised or informalised, and often involving working for co-ethnic employers. While the grey labour economies they occupied were tenuous spaces for all workers, migrant and local alike, temporary status and the desire to stay in Australia created specific types of vulnerabilities.

For example, because 485 and 417 workers often can't get jobs through regular recruitment channels, they rely heavily on social connections: fellow temporary migrants, family friends, church members, housemates, and landlords are common sources of finding employment. This can place them in a space of social obligation in the workplace and further magnifies the power asymmetries between the worker and the employee. A Chinese graduate of a research master's degree, for example, told me that he struggled to find full-time work after graduating but was offered a casual research assistant role at his old university by his former thesis supervisor. The complex power dynamic created by their previous academic relationship, however, made navigating the workplace relationship extremely difficult. When the worker found he was not being paid for many of the hours worked, he quit the job rather than confront his boss and former supervisor or report the underpayment to HR.

The following narrative of a female Chinese 485 worker further illustrates some of the complex power dynamics at play, specifically in co-ethnic employment. She worked in an administrative role for a medium-sized business owned by a Chinese permanent migrant, who employed mostly Chinese temporary workers.

---

34   Cate Gribble and Jill Blackmore, 'Re-positioning Australia's International Education in Global Knowledge Economies: Implications of Shifts in Skilled Migration Policies for Universities' (2012) 34(4) *Journal of Higher Education Policy and Management* 341.

The owner of the company is actually from my city in China. So we know each other pretty well and he actually provides me a job and he promised me that he can sponsor me to migrate … I was feeling like I was really happy but he said, 'I can't really pay you much. Probably $10 an hour in the beginning,' and I was like, 'That's okay.' So that's the reason I actually agreed to work for him and the low wage. After six months, I feel like he doesn't mention it at all and actually asked me to apply for ABN [Australian Business Number] number because he doesn't want to pay tax for me. So I actually got a feeling, 'This is just a lie.' That's when I quit my job. When I worked there, I actually planned to migrate here through the employment and sponsorship.

The lure of sponsorship as a pay-off for underpayment or poor working conditions and coercions by employers into semi-compliance was a very common story. Co-ethnic employers had further capacity to do this because they had a certain level of trust with the workers,[35] or workers had had little success securing mainstream employment. NGOs working with these groups reported that, while a lack of knowledge of rights and entitlements was sometimes an issue, it was more common that workers were, like in the example above, initially willing to trade rights for opportunities,[36] or that they were too afraid to complain or report breaches.

Taiwanese 417 workers, for example, talked openly about 'white' (legal) and 'black' (illegal) jobs, also sharing information amongst themselves about which employers they should be wary of. Reporting non-compliance not only had risks for the workers, but for their similarly precarious co-workers. Threats of being reported to immigration for not adhering to the requirements of their visas were also sometimes used by employers to make workers even more reluctant to report.

There are various 'lines of difference'[37] within 417 and 485 worker communities that have specific bearing on labour market experiences. Workers with limited English skills (most likely to be recently arrived 417 workers from countries such as Korea and Taiwan) were across-the-board more likely to be in grey labour and subject to exploitation. Yet, as the above examples have shown, even skilled, white, English-speaking migrants were subject to exploitation because of

35   Selvaraj Velayutham, above fn 31.
36   Cate Gribble and Jill Blackmore, above fn 34; Shanthi Robertson, above fn 6.
37   Nick Clarke, 'Detailing Transnational Lives of the Middle: British Working Holiday Makers in Australia' (2005) 31 *Journal of Ethnic and Migration Studies* 307.

their temporary status and their desire to stay. Clearly, for 417 and 485 workers, as with most temporary migrants, temporary status itself creates forms of 'differential inclusion',[38] particularly in terms of vulnerabilities in the workplace, as 'temporariness ... embeds and normalises a directionality in which workers' rights are limited and states' rights (to expel, to control) are expanded'.[39]

Social relations and the transformation of settler-citizen society

The position of 417 and 485 workers at the boundaries between long-term and short-term, temporary and permanent, sits in uncomfortable ambiguity with ideas of community and belonging, and has significant potential consequences for social relations. This is particularly the case in the Australian context where migration has, since the post-war era, largely been framed around linear and permanent journeys from alien to citizen, and arrival to assimilation. All kinds of migration create 'historical discontinuities in collective identities',[40] but 'mutant mobilities' like workers on 417 and 485 visas, in particular, disturb meanings of ethnic community and national belonging that have been built around settler-citizen migrant identities. Ethnic communities in settler societies such as Australia, Canada, and New Zealand have always had levels of internal heterogeneity, based on religion, class, regional, and linguistic difference, and on the different 'types' (skilled/unskilled/humanitarian/family) or historical 'waves' of migration from specific source countries and regions. Mutant mobilities, with their inherent temporal uncertainties, create another layer of heterogeneity within communities based on the unstable temporal barrier between the 'temporary' and the 'permanent' migrant.

---

38   Stephen Castles, 'How Nation-States Respond to Immigration and Ethnic Diversity' (1995) 21 *New Community: The Journal of the European Research Centre on Migration and Ethnic Relations* 293; Tim Creswell, 'The Prosthetic Citizen: New Geographies of Citizenship' (2009) 20 *Political Power and Social Theory* 259; Deepa Rajkumar et al., 'At the Temporary-Permanent Divide: How Canada Produces Temporariness and Makes Citizens through Its Security, Work, and Settlement Policies' (2012) 16 *Citizenship Studies* 483; James Walsh, 'Quantifying Citizens: Neoliberal Restructuring and Immigrant Selection in Canada and Australia' (2011) 15 *Citizenship Studies* 861.

39   Catherine Dauvergne and Sarah Marsden, 'The Ideology of Temporary Labour Migration in the Post-Global Era' (2014) 18(2) *Citizenship Studies* 224.

40   Rainer Bauböck, 'Sharing History and Future?' (1998) 4 *Constellations* 320.

Previous research in Australia on student-migrants and tourist-workers has begun to reveal complexities around their embeddedness within local communities, often describing tensions or ambivalent relationships between established and temporary groups.[41] Other work shows that long-term temporary migrants can also live in a segregated sub-cultural space, mostly only interacting with other temporary migrants of their own nationality.[42] The 485 and 417 workers can also find themselves temporally excluded from diaspora and transnational social fields because, as Saulo Cwerner argues, diaspora community is associated with long-term settlement and commitment, and this can come into tension with the real or perceived 'short-termism' of temporary migrants within existing ethnic community structures.[43]

The tensions and segregations around the boundaries of temporariness and permanence were very much apparent in the social worlds of the participants in this study. The fact that permanent migrants often played the role of corrupt employers, as described above, created part of this tension, but there was also the general sense that the temporary and permanent groups led largely separate lives and had little in common. The 417 and 485 workers relied on each other for information about jobs, dealing with immigration and other issues related to their temporary status — experiences with which settler-migrants could not identify. The fact that most social networks were built through work and study, where colleagues and classmates were also often temporary, also meant that opportunities to meet people outside of these groups was often limited. Two Chinese 485 workers explained that most of their social networks were with other temporary migrants:

> I must say there's a little gap between the temporary and the permanent … Most of my friends, they are only on a student visa or temporary residency and I can feel there is a barrier between these two groups of people, actually, so it's really hard to identify.

---

41   See, for example, Supriya Singh and Anuja Cabraal, 'Indian Student Migrants in Australia: Issues of Community Sustainability' (2010) 18 *People and Place* 19; Gil-Soo Han, 'The Koreans in Sydney' (2010) 2 *Sydney Journal*.
42   Aprad Maksay, 'Japanese Working Holiday Makers in Australia: Subculture and Resistance' (2007) 11(1) *Tourism Review International* 33; Fiona Allon and Kay Anderson, above fn 6.
43   Saulo Cwerner, 'The Times of Migration' (2001) 27 *Journal of Ethnic and Migration Studies* 7.

> Most of my friends are Chinese [temporary migrants]. My classmates, and some of them friends that I met at work ... Most of my friends are from same background. Not even Australian-born Chinese because they're just Australian because we don't have much to talk about. We don't have same background. Actually, I want to make friends with them, but it's really hard.

Some 417 participants, however, also sought to distance themselves socially from other 417 workers, particularly from the backpacker culture associated with the more short-term and leisure-oriented groups. Older 417 workers seeking professional work experience and the chance at permanent migration wanted to be disassociated from some of the negative connotations around the backpacker stereotype of illegal work and party culture. Professional 417 workers distanced themselves from these identities by not living in backpacker hotspots such as the Sydney beachside suburbs of Coogee and Bondi, and not participating in social activities within the backpacker community. They instead socialised with other 417 workers who identified more as migrants and professionals, and tried to build networks within the local community.

Generally, the longer 417 and 485 workers stayed in Australia, the more likely they were to put down roots and build connections with permanent migrant communities and the Australian-born. However, until permanent migration status was secured, these relationships often had an inherent sense of tenuousness. Even when migrants subjectively felt socially and culturally rooted, the insecurity of not having permanent legal status caused significant anxiety and frustration around the possible eventuality of forced return, as well as the lack of formal recognition of their belonging and their contributions to Australian society:

> To be honest because in my occupation Australia needs lots of people in this field, but I can't do it [find a job], sometimes it's very frustrating to get a permanent residency. So I feel it's unfair and we spend a lot of money and we got good occupation, we can contribute our knowledge to this country, but we still feel frustrated to [stay] here ... It's still very strict to immigrate [permanently] here, so it is frustrating.

> When you put a lot of energy into building-up a network, you build-up like friends that you studied with and potentially work with. Like it's a lot of energy that you put in to this new career, this new life or

whatever it is and that they [the Immigration Department] can just change like this. It makes it hard because you need to plan. So that was really s**t, to be honest.

The mobility across different cities and regions required to seek out suitable employment and sponsorship opportunities also meant that migrants sometimes did not stay in the same place long enough to build lasting networks. Yet networks and relationships with permanent members of the community were often crucial to the success of a transition from temporary to permanent migrant. For those 417 and 485 workers seeking a longer or more permanent stay, local networks, either co-ethnic or within the broader community, could lead to job or sponsorship opportunities, spouse visas, or other forms of direct and indirect support that become crucial to meeting state criteria for longer-term membership.

In the case of any group with a historic pattern of settler-migration, existing family or social connections within the permanent local community often shaped migration trajectories and experiences in various ways. For example, extended family or kinship networks sometimes provided an incentive to migrate to a particular city or region, and could provide accommodation or employment support at different times. Yet connections within the community of other temporary migrants were also vital to most 417 and 485 workers to building the kinds of social capital that they specifically require for status mobility and extended stays, such as finding jobs to fit the requirements of gaining a sponsored visa, finding a migration agent, or navigating changes to immigration policies. Online communities were quite significant here, with 417 and 485 workers accessing a plethora of websites and forums dedicated to potential and current temporary migrants. They used these sites to seek advice and share experiences, including advice on finding accommodation, recommendations for migration agents and warnings about 'dodgy' employers.

Unintended consequences?

Overall, there are several major consequences of hidden labour migration streams such as 417 and 485 workers. These schemes create very complex mobilities that intertwine labour, tourism and education; but despite official rhetoric, labour and longer-term migration seem to be a core focus of many of these migrants' journeys. In addition, the implicit and explicit restrictions surrounding being temporary in the Australian labour market mean that goals and engagements with work and study often need to be reconfigured through deskilling, reskilling, labour market mobility, physical mobility into regional areas, and semi-compliance. As well as having specific vulnerabilities in the workplace, 417 and 485 workers also occupy an ambiguous place in terms of their embeddedness within both ethnic communities and the broader Australian community.

In governance discourses in Australia, temporariness is presented as 'a neutral policy objective':[44] a means to provide a flexible, demand-driven and expendable labour force to fill specific skills gaps while ameliorating populist concerns about permanent immigration, population control, and social cohesion. Schemes like the 417 and 485 visas allow an influx of migrant workers to exist alongside a state performance of 'border preservation',[45] as well as a performance of an overall migration program that is highly selective and only accepts elite and highly skilled workers. The disassociation of 417 and 485 mobilities from labour migration, and the ongoing positioning of these workers within transient consumer student and backpacker identities, furthers the presentation of these temporary schemes as 'neutral' and 'unproblematic'. The ongoing moral panic about asylum seekers that dominate the policy space also serve to keep these schemes less visible and outside of mainstream political discourse and public scrutiny. This is part of what Chris Wright refers to as the 'control dilemmas' of migration governance.[46] These visas also serve a double neoliberal purpose in that they shore up the lucrative international education and tourism markets, while simultaneously, and largely covertly, supplying streams of flexible temporary labour into various industries and specific regions, creating a cheap and exploitable workforce with no access to social welfare and limited access to rights.

---

44   Catherine Dauvergne and Sarah Marsden, above fn 39.

45   Gail Lewis, 'Introduction: Contemporary Political Contexts, Changing Terrains and Revisited Discourses' (2005) 28 *Ethnic and Racial Studies* 423.

46   Chris Wright, 'How Do States Implement Liberal Immigration Policies?: Control Signals and Skilled Immigration Reform in Australia' (2013) 27(3) *Governance* 397.

These labour and economic effects of 417 and 485 schemes are not able to be assessed as part of the 'unintended consequences'[47] that inevitably surround attempts to govern migration. They quite clearly serve very particular economic and political agendas, and recent extensions of these schemes in policy reveal quite purposeful attempts to expand these streams of labour while continuing with discourses that render them invisible *as* labour. What is perhaps less intentional are some of the complex social and political consequences and questions drawn out by these mutant mobilities in the context of Australia's history as a settler-citizen society, some of which are outlined in more detail by Peter Mares in the next chapter. With overall temporary intakes beginning to equal or surpass permanent migrant intakes, temporary migrant workers represent Australia's future cultural diversity and new formations of migrant community. Yet the ambiguity around transience and permanence inherent in their migration experiences makes their position in Australia and their relationships to their countries of origin markedly different from previous waves of settler-migrants. These issues present a number of policy challenges around migration governance, settlement services, and labour market engagement. The relatively small-scale research discussed here already unveils a significant number of these challenges. Further research into the work and life experiences of these workers is crucial to ensuring the success of these migration programs, and to ensuring policy development is informed by nuanced understandings of migrant experiences and the wider social and cultural impact of policy.

Bibliography

Allon, Fiona and Kay Anderson, 'Intimate Encounters: The Embodied Transnationalism of Backpackers and Independent Travellers' (2010) 16 *Population, Space and Place* 11

Allon, Fiona, Kay Anderson and Robyn Bushell, 'Mutant Mobilities: Backpacker Tourism in "Global" Sydney' (2008) 3 *Mobilities* 73

Baas, Michiel, *Imagined Mobility: Migration and Transnationalism Among Indian Students in Australia* (Anthem Press, 2010)

---

47   Stephen Castles, above fn 9.

Bauböck, Rainer, 'Sharing History and Future?' (1998) 4 *Constellations* 320

Birrell, Bob and Earnest Healy, 'Immigration Overshoot' (Centre for Population and Urban Research Report, Monash University, 2012)

Castles, Stephen, 'How Nation-States Respond to Immigration and Ethnic Diversity' (1995) 21 *New Community* 293

Castles, Stephen, 'Migration and Community Formation under Conditions of Globalization' (2002) 36 *International Migration Review* 1143

Castles, Stephen, 'The Factors That Make and Unmake Migration Policies' (2004) 38 *International Migration Review* 852

Clarke, Nick, 'Detailing Transnational Lives of the Middle: British Working Holiday Makers in Australia' (2005) 31 *Journal of Ethnic and Migration Studies* 307

Creswell, Tim, 'The Prosthetic Citizen: New Geographies of Citizenship' (2009) 20 *Political Power and Social Theory* 259

Cwerner, Saulo, 'The Times of Migration' (2001) 27 *Journal of Ethnic and Migration Studies* 7

Dauvergne, Catherine and Sarah Marsden, 'The Ideology of Temporary Labour Migration in the Post-Global Era' (2014) 18(2) *Citizenship Studies* 224

Department of Immigration and Citizenship, *Temporary Entrants and New Zealand Citizens in Australia* (2012). Available at: www.border.gov.au/ReportsandPublications/Documents/statistics/temp-entrants-newzealand-dec12.pdf

Department of Immigration and Citizenship, 'Record Interest in Australia's Visitor Visa Programs' (2013). Available at: migrationblog.border.gov.au/2013/03/01/record-interest-in-australias-visitor-visa-programs/

Department of Immigration and Citizenship, *Visas, Immigration and Refugees: Working Holiday* (2013). Available at: www.border.gov.au/ReportsandPublications/Documents/statistics/working-holiday-report-jun13.pdf

Department of Immigration and Citizenship, *Working Holiday Maker Visa Program Report* (30 June 2013). Available at: www.border. gov.au/ReportsandPublications/Documents/statistics/working-holiday-report-jun13.pdf

Findlay, A M, 'From Settlers to Skilled Transients: The Changing Structure of British International Migration' (1988) 19(4) *Geoforum* 401

Gribble, Cate and Jill Blackmore, 'Re-positioning Australia's International Education in Global Knowledge Economies: Implications of Shifts in Skilled Migration Policies for Universities' (2012) 34(4) *Journal of Higher Education Policy and Management* 341

Guthrie, Robert, 'Tourists Overstaying Their Welcome: When the Visa Runs Out and the Workers Stay On' (2004) 6 *The Tourism Industry* 22

Han, Gil-Soo, 'The Koreans in Sydney' (2010) 2 *Sydney Journal*

Hugo, Graeme, 'In and Out of Australia' (2008) 4 *Asian Population Studies* 267

Jang, Haeyoung, Kyungja Jung and Bronwen Dalton, 'Factors Influencing Labour Migration of Korean Women into the Entertainment and Sex Industry in Australia' (Paper presented at 6th Biennial Korean Studies Association of Australasia, University of Sydney, 8–9 July 2009)

Kenney, Ciara, 'Canada Doubles Quota of Irish Working Holiday Visas', *The Irish Times*, 6 October 2012. Available at: www.irishtimes. com/news/canada-doubles-quota-of-irish-working-holiday-visas-1.548331

Khoo, Siew-Ean and Graeme Hugo, 'Which Skilled Temporary Migrants Become Permanent Residents and Why?' (2008) 42 *International Migration Review* 193

Knight, Michael, 'Strategic Review of the Student Visa Program' (Report to the Australian Government, June 2011)

Landolt, Patricia and Lurin Goldring, 'Caught in the Work–Citizenship Matrix: The Lasting Effects of Precarious Legal Status on Work for Toronto Immigrants' (2011) 8 *Globalizations* 325

Lawson, Victoria, 'Arguments Within Geographies of Movement: The Theoretical Potential of Migrants' Stories' (2000) 24 *Progress in Human Geography* 173

Lewis, Gail, 'Introduction: Contemporary Political Contexts, Changing Terrains and Revisited Discourses' (2005) 28 *Ethnic and Racial Studies* 423

Madden, Marie, 'Galway's "Gathering" Down Under', *Galway Independent*, 13 March 2013

Maksay, Aprad, 'Japanese Working Holiday Makers in Australia: Subculture and Resistance' (2007) 11(1) *Tourism Review International* 33

Mares, Peter, 'Temporary Migration and Its Implications for Australia' (speech to the Australian Senate, 23 September 2011). Available at: www.aph.gov.au/About_Parliament/Senate/Powers_practice_n_ procedures/~/media/FB57E1420B9748698CCB4B84A799F08D.ashx

Mares, Peter, 'Graduate Visas May Yet Prove Controversial' *The Age*, 4 April 2013. Available at: www.theage.com.au/comment/ graduate-visas-may-yet-prove-controversial-20130403-2h706. html#ixzz314WqNveK

Ong, Aihwa, 'Mutations in Citizenship' (2006) 23(2–3) *Theory, Culture and Society* 499

O'Neill, Luke, '"Deep Recession" Cited in Irish Man's Visa Review', *Irish Echo*, 18 March 2011. Available at: www.irishecho. com.au/2011/03/18/deep-recession-cited-in-irish-mans-visa-review/8150

Rajkumar, Deepa, Laurel Berkowitz, Leah F. Vosko, Valerie Preston and Robert Latham, 'At the Temporary-Permanent Divide: How Canada Produces Temporariness and Makes Citizens through its Security, Work, and Settlement Policies' (2012) 16 *Citizenship Studies* 483

Robertson, Shanthi, 'Cash Cows, Backdoor Migrants, or Activist Citizens? International Students, Citizenship, and Rights in Australia' (2011) 34 *Ethnic and Racial Studies* 2192

Robertson, Shanthi, *Transnational Student-Migrants and the State: The Education–Migration Nexus* (Palgrave Macmillan, 2013)

Robertson, Shanthi, 'Time and Temporary Migration: The Case of Temporary Graduate Workers and Working Holiday Makers in Australia' (2014) 40(12) *Journal of Ethnic and Migration Studies* 1915

Ruhs, Martin, 'The Potential of Temporary Migration Programmes in Future International Migration Policy' (2006) 145(1–2) *International Labour Review* 7

Ruhs, Martin, *The Price of Rights: Regulating International Labor Migration* (Princeton University Press, 2013)

Ruhs, Martin and Bridget Anderson, 'Semi-Compliance and Illegality in Migrant Labour Markets: An Analysis of Migrants, Employers and the State in the UK' (2010) 16 *Population, Space and Place* 195

Schuster, Liza, 'The Continuing Mobility of Migrants in Italy: Shifting Between Places and Statuses' (2005) 31 *Journal of Ethnic and Migration Studies* 757

Singh, Supriya and Anuja Cabraal, 'Indian Student Migrants in Australia: Issues of Community Sustainability' (2010) 18 *People and Place* 19

Tan, Yan and Laurence Hester, 'Labour Market and Economic Impacts of International Working Holiday Temporary Migrants to Australia' (2011) 18 *Population, Space and Place* 359

Toh, Stefanie and Michael Quinlan, 'Safeguarding the Global Contingent Workforce?: Guestworkers in Australia' (2009) 30 *International Journal of Manpower* 453

Velayutham, Selvaraj, 'Precarious Experiences of Indians in Australia on 457 Temporary Work Visas' (2013) 24 *The Economic and Labour Relations Review* 340

Walsh, James, 'Quantifying Citizens: Neoliberal Restructuring and Immigrant Selection in Canada and Australia' (2011) 15 *Citizenship Studies* 861

Wright, Chris, 'How Do States Implement Liberal Immigration Policies?: Control Signals and Skilled Immigration Reform in Australia' (2013) 27(3) *Governance* 397

Yeoh, Brenda, Katie Willis and Abdul Fakhri, 'Introduction: Transnationalism and its Edges' (2003) 26(2) *Ethnic and Racial Studies* 207

4

Unintended Consequences of Temporary Migration to Australia

Peter Mares

Introduction

Some unintended consequences of temporary migration are well-known. For example, under the Howard Government, linking certain courses of tertiary study in Australia with almost automatic permanent residency led to a dramatic increase in student enrolments in newly created private colleges offering the shortest route to permanent migration; this overwhelmed the permanent skilled migration program, with qualified applicants far outnumbering the places available in the system.[1]

Another familiar example is the way in which employer sponsorship for permanent residency risks making temporary migrant workers on 457 visas more vulnerable to workplace exploitation. This was examined in Barbara Deegan's 2008 review of the integrity of the 457 visa system.[2]

---

1   See, for example, Peter Mares, 'Lives On Hold', *Inside Story*, 2 May 2011. Available at: insidestory.org.au/lives-on-hold/.
2   Barbara Deegan, 'Visa Subclass 457 Integrity Review: Final Report' (2008). Available at: www.immi.gov.au/skilled/skilled-workers/_pdf/457-integrity-review.pdf.

This chapter takes familiarity with these recognised unintended consequences of temporary migration as a given and aims to present some less well-known examples. The examples are chosen not just because they are interesting in their own right, but also because they serve to illustrate a broader point — namely, that the increased use of temporary migration as a tool of policy raises moral and practical issues that Australia as a society and a polity is yet to recognise or address.

In the previous chapter, Shanthi Robertson observed that 'norms around migration are arguably still embedded within a "settler-citizen" paradigm, and understandings of temporary migrant experiences are particularly limited'. This chapter seeks to build on Robertson's insight in two ways. Firstly, it argues that just as the norms around migration remain embedded in an outdated paradigm, so too do administrative and legal structures, with the result that long term temporary migrants with work rights often find themselves falling into cracks in the system. These are the unintended consequences referred to in the title and illustrated in the examples below. Secondly, this chapter argues that an updated policy approach (and updated legal and administrative systems) must be based on updated norms, more appropriate to the new realities of Australia's migration program and the large role that temporary migration now plays in it. In this regard I draw on Joseph Carens' arguments about the moral impact of the passage of time on a receiving state's obligations towards temporary migrants, and use this to critique existing policy settings in Australia and to gesture at potential alternative approaches.

The fundamental argument is that, over time, questions around access to specific rights and entitlements for migrant workers — such as workplace protections or access to government services — ultimately resolve themselves into a question of political membership. In other words, they inevitably lead to the 'threshold' question: at what point does, or should, 'temporary' become 'permanent'?

This chapter cites examples of the unintended consequences of temporary migration as they play out in individual lives. These stories are based primarily on interviews and other materials gathered by the author in his capacity as a journalist.[3] To put these stories in context, the chapter also assembles publicly available immigration department data to document the statistical significance of the rise in temporary migration to Australia in recent years.

The false divide between temporary and permanent migration

Policy-makers are want to present temporary migration as a neat and tidy affair that is quite distinct from permanent migration, as if they were two 'quite separate and unrelated processes'.[4] This sentiment was evident in the words of Scott Morrison, the first Minister for Immigration in the Abbott Government, in a speech made when he was in Opposition:

> We must be careful to manage the population impacts of … temporary migration, ensuring that we apply appropriate constraints, most importantly that such entrants return home when their purpose and stay has been completed — whether it is to work, study or visit — without onward application entitlements.[5]

Temporary migrants are expected to come to Australia, go about their business and then leave when their visa expires. Unfortunately for politicians, migration is an inherently messy process. As Dauvergne and Marsden note, while 'workers [or students] may be invited, it is human beings who arrive'.[6] Over time, the boundaries between what constitutes a temporary stay and what constitutes longer-term engagement with the nation and the society tend to blur, especially

---

3   The author is currently contributing editor to the online news and culture magazine *Inside Story*, where many of his articles on temporary migration have appeared. Prior to 2012, he reported on these issues on *The National Interest* program on ABC Radio National.

4   Siew-Ean Khoo, Graeme Hugo and Peter McDonald, 'Which Skilled Temporary Migrants Become Permanent Residents and Why?' (2008) 42 *International Migration Review* 193.

5   Scott Morrison, 'Our Nation' (Address to the 2011 Federation of Ethnic Community Councils of Australia Conference, Adelaide, 18 November 2011). Available at: australianpolitics. com/2011/11/18/morrison-promises-to-protect-the-borders-of-our-values.html#more-4574.

6   Catherine Dauvergne and Sarah Marsden, 'The Ideology of Temporary Labour Migration in the Post-Global Era' (2014) 18 *Citizenship Studies* 225. This reformulates the famous 1965 observation by Swiss playwright Max Frisch in relation to Italian guest workers: '*Man hat Arbeitskräfte gerufen, und es kamen Menschen.*' (We called for labour power and human beings came.)

when a temporary stay is constructed in policy terms — as is increasingly the case in Australia — as a potential first step towards permanency.[7]

The biggest unintended consequence of temporary migration is, arguably, that the more time migrants spend living, working, and studying in Australia, the more financial, cultural, psychological, and emotional attachments they are likely to develop. (This process is appropriately described as putting down roots. After a short time the roots will be shallow. After a longer period, they will reach deeper.) As a result, these temporary migrants also accumulate rights — moral rights, if not legal ones. Consequently, we as citizens, via the government that represents us, also accumulate obligations towards temporary migrants.

As documented in more detail below, the number of temporary migrants present in Australia has been growing steadily since the mid-1990s, with developments such as the introduction of the 457 temporary work visa, the expansion of the 'Working Holiday Maker' scheme, the internationalisation of Australia's education system, and changes to the status of New Zealanders living in Australia. What is more, it is now becoming apparent that increasing numbers of temporary migrants are renewing their visas or moving sequentially from one temporary visa subclass to another temporary visa subclass. This opens up the possibility for temporary migrants to be lawfully present in Australia and to be active and engaged members of Australian society for years at a time, without necessarily moving down a pathway to Australian residency or Australian citizenship, and the rights and entitlements that come with such status.

This poses new political and ethical questions for society. Carens has summarised the conundrum neatly by asking if there is a place for such long-term temporary migrants on the 'normative map' of liberal democracy.[8] Neither short-term visitors nor permanent residents, these migrants work and study, pay taxes and university fees, abide

---

7   For a discussion on how the 457 temporary skilled worker visa is now a fundamental component of the process for selecting permanent migrants, see, for example, Peter Mares, 'Temporary Migration is a Permanent Thing', *Inside Story*, 20 March 2013. Available at: inside. org.au/temporary-migration-is-a-permanent-thing/.
8   Joseph H Carens, 'Live-in Domestics, Seasonal Workers, and Others Hard to Locate on the Map of Democracy' (2008) 16 *The Journal of Political Philosophy* 419, 420.

by laws and contribute to the economic and cultural life of the nation in myriad other ways. Carens asks whether liberal democracies should be able to admit people to their societies in this way, 'without putting them on a path to citizenship and without granting them most of the rights that citizens enjoy'?[9] His answer (framed as a question of justice, rather than political pragmatism) inclines towards a 'no'. When combined with 'the moral importance of the passage of time', he argues that both 'the inner logic of democracy and a commitment to liberal principles require the full inclusion of the entire settled population', because 'the longer the stay, the stronger the claim to full membership in society and to the enjoyment of the same rights as citizens, including, eventually, citizenship itself'.[10]

As Shanthi Robertson has observed in relation to international students, the rise of temporary migration is 'radically different to the trend of permanent settler migration' that characterised Australian policy in the second half of the twentieth century.[11] As a result, 'paradigms of settlement, permanent residency and full citizenship ... are being destabilised'.[12] Yet to date, the important questions raised by Carens have not engaged the attention of many Australian policy-makers or theorists.[13]

In fact, we even lack the appropriate language to discuss these issues. The term 'guest worker' (or *Gastarbeiter*) with its specific historical connotations and references is clearly inadequate to encompass a range of temporary migrants that includes both high-skilled professionals and undergraduate students. Like the term 'sojourner',[14] it also implies a degree of temporariness that assumes return and does not accord with the emerging reality of '"staggered" migration processes, characterised by multiple "gates" of membership that migrants must pass through to enter the nation state'.[15] An alternative

---

9   Ibid., 419.
10   Ibid.
11   Shanthi Robertson, *Transnational Student-Migrants and the State: The Education-Migration Nexus* (Palgrave Macmillan, 2013) 1.
12   Ibid., 166.
13   There are exceptions, including notably, Shanthi Robertson, above fn 11; Joo-Cheong Tham, 'Multiculturalism and Temporary Migration: Where Does Justice Fit?' (Presentation to Australian Multicultural Commission roundtable, Melbourne, 15 March 2013).
14   Shanthi Robertson, above fn 11, 41.
15   Ibid., 68.

that is sometimes offered is 'denizens', while Michael Walzer compares such long-term temporary residents to the *metics* of ancient Athens, foreigners in the city who were neither citizens nor slaves.[16]

For reasons of clarity, this chapter refers to 'long-term temporary migrants with work rights', thus encompassing international students and working holiday makers, as well as migrant workers on 457 visas. It is a rather clumsy formulation and even here the language is potentially inadequate since reference is also made to New Zealanders, whose Special Category Visas (SCVs) render their presence in Australia as neither temporary nor permanent, but rather indefinite.[17] (As outlined below, however, the SCV is classified as a temporary visa in migration law.)

Example 1: Temporary migrants and workers' compensation

When 34-year-old English nurse Claire Hewitt migrated to the Northern Territory (NT) in 2009, it was no rash or random decision. Together with her photographer husband, Terry, she had spent the previous year travelling around Australia in a campervan and had fallen in love with the outback. After having a good look around, the couple decided where they wanted to go and what they wanted to do.[18]

As a registered nurse, Hewitt could have found a job in Sydney or Melbourne, but she reckons that would have been little different to working in a clinic in London. She says she wanted to do something that she could not do anywhere else.

The couple settled in Alice Springs so Hewitt could take up a job with the NT Government working on a trachoma treatment and prevention program in remote Aboriginal communities.

---

16 Michael Walzer, *Spheres of Justice: A Defense of Pluralism and Equality* (Basic Books, 1983) 53.

17 For discussion of whether the SCV is a temporary or permanent visa, see David Faulkner, 'The Unequal Treatment of New Zealanders in Australia' (2013). Available at: papers.ssrn.com/sol3/papers.cfm?abstract_id=2304476.

18 Interview with Claire Hewitt (29 August 2013). The following outline of Claire Hewitt's story is based on the above interview, which was conducted as research for the following article: Peter Mares, 'Falling Between the Cracks of Temporary Migration', *Inside Story*, 1 November 2013. Available at: inside.org.au/falling-between-the-cracks-of-temporary-migration/. (The article was provided to Ms Hewitt for fact checking prior to publication and published with her permission.)

This is important work. Trachoma is an easily treatable and easily preventable eye disease and is the leading cause of infectious blindness in 59 of the world's poorest countries. Australia is the only developed country in the world to still have active trachoma in remote Indigenous communities.[19]

If it had been possible, the couple would have migrated to Australia on a permanent visa, perhaps under the Employer Nomination or Regional Sponsored Migration Scheme. However, NT authorities told Hewitt that they had had bad experiences with permanent skilled migration: new arrivals would often be unprepared for local conditions and quickly decamp to a larger city in another part of Australia with a less extreme climate. She says the NT health department encouraged her to come on a 457 visa instead.[20] She was given to understand that if she liked the work and the lifestyle, then, after 12 months, the department would sponsor her for permanent residency.

Hewitt and her husband were in the middle of doing the paperwork for that application when she had her accident.

On 18 May 2010, while driving to the remote community of Mt Leibig, Hewitt rolled her car six times. She was lucky to survive after being trapped in the vehicle for a long time and receiving massive head injuries, 33 fractures to her chest, and severe nerve damage to both arms.

Hewitt was hospitalised for three months and underwent major surgery, including a procedure to transfer her pectoral muscle from her chest to her shoulder to restore her ability to raise her left arm. It was an operation performed only once before in Australia. Eighteen-months of full-time rehabilitation followed and, three years later, much of Hewitt's routine still revolves around appointments with therapists and specialists. Since the accident, her husband Terry has been devoted almost full-time to her care.

---

19   Melbourne School of Population and Global Health, Indigenous Eye Health Unit, *The Trachoma Story Kit*. Available at: iehu.unimelb.edu.au/the_trachoma_story_kit/introduction.

20   This approach was presumably based on the assumption that labour mobility amongst temporary 457 visa holders is lower than amongst permanent residents (due to the fact that a temporary migrant's visa status is linked to ongoing employment with an eligible sponsor).

It is a nightmare story, but Hewitt's recovery has astounded her doctors. The rehabilitation specialist consulting on her case, Associate Professor Les Koopowitz from the University of Adelaide, commented that Hewitt 'continues to attain the type of progress seldom realised following such a serious, devastating and debilitating accident'.[21]

As a result of the crash, Hewitt expects to have a lifetime of disability, pain, and medical conditions. She accepts that she cannot return to her old job in remote communities, but is nevertheless determined to return to nursing in some capacity. 'Right from the beginning they almost had to hold me down to stop me trying to go back to work', she said. 'In a way I haven't helped myself. I tried to do too much too soon. My brain has to relearn things and that takes time.'[22]

Hewitt says that throughout her long rehabilitation, the NT Department of Health assured her that it would fully support her eventual return to work, including tailoring her duties to her abilities where necessary.

In mid-2013, however, everything changed when the department indicated that it would no longer sponsor her application for a permanent visa. This made it likely that she would have to leave Australia when her temporary 457 visa expired in June 2014.

The implications for Hewitt were profound. If Hewitt had to leave Australia, then she would lose access to the extensive medical and rehabilitation team that have worked with her for the past three years. As a result, she would probably also lose any realistic chance of returning to her career as a nurse.

Professor Koopowitz argues that Hewitt's ongoing recovery is highly dependent on 'continuity of care and environmental stability', and that undermining this could seriously compromise her ongoing recovery and render hopes of a return to any meaningful work 'an unrealistic challenge'.

At the time of her crash, Hewitt was at work and driving a government vehicle. In other words, it was a workplace accident, and Hewitt was covered by workers' compensation. NT Workcover pays her medical bills, and she continues to receive 75 per cent of her salary.

---

21   Email from Les Koopowitz to the author (23 October 2013).
22   Interview with Claire Hewitt, above fn 18.

The NT Workers Rehabilitation and Compensation Act states that:

> *rehabilitation* means the process necessary to ensure, as far as is practicable, having regard to community standards from time to time, that an injured worker is restored to the same physical, economic and social condition in which the worker was before suffering the relevant injury.[23]

The Act makes no reference to a worker's visa status. There has never before been a case like Hewitt's under the NT scheme.

Hewitt's legal advice is that if she has to leave Australia and return to the UK, then medical bills relating to her accident will still be paid by the compensation scheme. Her salary entitlements, however, are a different matter.

If Hewitt were a permanent resident and unable to return to work full-time, or at the same pay level as at the time of her accident, then the workers' compensation scheme would top up her salary so that her original income was maintained. In the event that Hewitt was unable to return to work at all, she would receive 75 per cent of her original salary. Either way, the entitlement would continue until the age of 67.

If, however, Hewitt leaves Australia, then her salary entitlements would cut out after two, or possibly, four years. After that time Hewitt would have to rely on UK government disability benefits.

Hewitt says the NT health department told her in 2013 that she no longer met the criteria for sponsorship as a skilled migrant. This may or may not have been true, but she wanted the department to sponsor her application even if it was doomed to failure, because she believed and was advised that her best hope of staying in Australia ultimately lay with ministerial intervention.[24] But there is a Catch 22 here: the immigration minister cannot use his discretion to intervene in a migration case (even when there are compelling and compassionate circumstances) until all other avenues of appeal have been exhausted. The minister's public interest power to substitute a decision that is more favourable to the applicant in migration cases requires 'a review tribunal decision to exist

---

23   *Workers Rehabilitation and Compensation Act* (NT) pt V div 4 (2). (Emphasis in original.)

24   Under the *Migration Act 1958* (Cth) s351(1), s417(1) and s501J(1), the minister may, in the public interest, substitute for a decision of a tribunal, a decision that is more favourable to the applicant.

before he can intervene'.[25] In the context of immigration decisions, a 'review tribunal' means 'the Refugee Review Tribunal (RRT), the Migration Review Tribunal (MRT) or, in certain circumstances, the Administrative Appeals Tribunal (AAT)'.[26] Unless the NT lodged an application that fails, Hewitt would have no decision to appeal to a tribunal and could not therefore seek ministerial intervention.

'Our lives are here', said Hewitt. 'We didn't come here with the intention of having a holiday, we moved ourselves lock, stock and barrel.'[27] And after all that Hewitt has been through, Australia is more home than ever.

After members of parliament and journalists drew public attention to Hewitt's case, the NT health department wrote to her advising that it would, after all, sponsor her application for a permanent visa. A visa was eventually granted in October 2014.[28]

Even though the eventual outcome for Hewitt was positive, the ad hoc arrangements reached in her particular case do not resolve the outstanding tensions and contradictions that gave rise to it in the first place.

Hewitt's predicament is one disturbing example of an unintended consequence of the rise of temporary migration in Australia. While her case is highly specific and personal, it is predictable, indeed likely, that similar cases will arise in future, since many of Australia's legal and institutional structures are based on the assumption that if people are not citizens or permanent residents of Australia, then they are here only as short-term visitors. Administrative and legal systems have not been designed to envisage a situation in which a significant and growing proportion of the population consists of people like Hewitt — long-term temporary migrants with work rights.

Such people cannot be simply and neatly defined. They are resident in Australia, but they are not, legally speaking, residents. It is the visas they hold that define their status, and since there are a range of different long-term temporary visas that come with permission

---

25 Department of Immigration and Border Protection, *Ministerial Intervention* (14 May 2014). Available at: www.immi.gov.au/refugee/ministerial_intervention.htm (site discontinued).

26 Ibid.

27 Interview with Claire Hewitt, above fn 18.

28 Email from Claire and Terry Hewitt to the author (10 February 2015).

to work, different cohorts within this group enjoy (or lack) different rights and entitlements. What can be said in general about this group is that they are all non-Australians, and that as their numbers grow, more of them will find themselves falling between legislative and regulatory cracks that were not previously apparent.

Example 2: Temporary migrants and the Fair Entitlements Guarantee

When Tony Abbott was Employment Minister in the Howard Government, he set up GEERS — the General Employee Entitlements and Redundancy Scheme. Its creation followed the collapse of a string of high-profile companies — One-Tel, HIH, Ansett, and National Textiles (a company run by John Howard's brother, Stan, that went bust leaving 342 workers with unpaid entitlements). GEERS is now known as FEG — the Fair Entitlements Guarantee — but its function remains essentially the same. It is a scheme to cover the unpaid wages and holiday entitlements of workers whose employer goes bankrupt.

In May 2013, the Swan Services Cleaning Group went into administration owing $2.3 million in unpaid wages and $7.2 million in annual leave entitlements to around 2,500 workers.[29] But many if not most of those workers will not qualify for payments under the FEG, because to be eligible under the Act a person must be 'an Australian citizen or, under the *Migration Act 1958*, the holder of a permanent visa or a special category visa'.[30]

A large proportion of the Swan Services workforce — about half of its staff in Victoria — was made up of international students. Many were left with up to three weeks' worth of unpaid wages, and some were owed close to $3,000.[31] Like Claire Hewitt, they have fallen into a regulatory crack where the government assistance extended to their fellow workers does not reach.

---

29   United Voice, *Swan Cleaning Services Update* (5 June 2013). Available at: www.unitedvoice. org.au/news/swan-cleaning-services-update.

30   *Fair Entitlements Guarantee Act 2012* (Cth) pt 2 div 1 sub-div A para 10 (1)(g). SCV holders are New Zealanders.

31   Madeleine Heffernan and Clay Lucas, 'International Students Taken to the Cleaners', *The Age*, 2 June 2013. Available at: www.theage.com.au/national/international-students-taken-to-the-cleaners-20130601-2nily.html#ixzz2iQHeVVzWwww.theage.com.au/national/international-students-taken-to-the-cleaners-20130601-2nily.html#ixzz2iQHeVVzW.

Example 3: New Zealanders

Many New Zealanders found themselves caught in a different regulatory gap during the devastating floods that hit Queensland in the summer of 2009–10. To help people get through the worst of the crisis, the Commonwealth Government authorised emergency funds for affected households of $1,000 per adult and $400 per child under the Australian Government Disaster Recovery Payment scheme. To be eligible for such payments, however, a person must meet the definition of 'Australian resident' under social security laws. Many long-term New Zealander residents were denied the emergency assistance because they had settled in Australia after 26 February 2001, when the *Family and Community Services Legislation Amendment (New Zealand citizens) Act 2001* came into force. The Act changed 'the definition of *Australian resident* for the purposes of the social security law', with the specific intention of 'restricting access to social security payments' for New Zealanders.[32]

The flood payments issue caused considerable controversy and media comment, as New Zealanders who had bought houses, and had children and established businesses in Australia were denied the same assistance as was offered to their neighbours. Many felt that they were being treated as 'second class citizens'.[33] A more accurate — though less catchy — complaint would have been that they were being treated as second-class *permanent residents*, since they had the right to reside and work indefinitely in Australia but did not have access to the same entitlements as other permanent residents.

Perceptions of Australian meanness at a time of need were amplified a few weeks later by the New Zealand Government's response to the 2011 Christchurch earthquake: Australians resident in that city were offered the same emergency and unemployment benefits as New Zealand citizens.[34]

---

32 Explanatory Memorandum, Family And Community Services Legislation Amendment (New Zealand Citizens) Bill 2001. (Emphasis in original.) On arrival in Australia, New Zealanders are automatically issued with a SCV that entitles them to work and live indefinitely in the country. New Zealanders resident in Australia prior to 2001 were exempt from the changes and are described as 'protected SCV holders'.

33 Hayden Donnell, 'New Zealand Pair Upset at Flood Cash "Racism"', *New Zealand Herald*, 21 January 2011. Available at: www.nzherald.co.nz/nz/news/article.cfm?c_id=1& objectid=10701102.

34 David Faulkner, above fn 17.

The outcry on both sides of the Tasman about the flood payments issue and official lobbying from Wellington eventually pressured the federal government into providing 'ex-gratia assistance payments' to New Zealanders who could demonstrate that they had been working in Australia for the three previous years.[35] This appears to have set a precedent that is now routinely repeated in response to other disasters. Similar ex-gratia payments have subsequently been made available to otherwise ineligible New Zealanders who were affected by the 2013 floods in Queensland[36] and NSW,[37] and by bushfires in October 2013 in NSW[38] and in January 2014 in WA.[39]

In response to recent disasters, the Commonwealth is also offering to pay an ex-gratia Income Support Allowance to New Zealanders who arrived in Australia after 26 February 2001 (and who are, therefore, ineligible for other forms of welfare such as unemployment benefits).[40]

Thus the situation as it stands is that eligibility for Australian Government Disaster Recovery Payments and emergency income support are restricted to those who qualify as residents for social security purposes, and exclude New Zealanders who arrived after 26 February 2001 and are therefore holders of non-protected SCVs. This is in line with the scope and intent of the 2001 amendments. Yet because the implications of this arrangement are politically and

---

35   New Zealand High Commission Canberra, Australia, *Floods Assistance*. Available at: www.nzembassy.com/australia/news/queensland-floods-assistance (site discontinued).

36   Department of Human Services, Australian Government, *Ex-Gratia Assistance for New Zealand Non-Protected Special Category Visa Holders: Queensland Floods January 2013*. Available at: www.humanservices.gov.au/spw/customer/forms/resources/em037-130212en.pdf (site discontinued).

37   Department of Human Services, Australian Government, *Ex-Gratia Assistance For New Zealand Non-Protected Special Category Visa Holders: New South Wales Floods January 2013*. Available at: www.humanservices.gov.au/spw/customer/forms/resources/em039-130215en.pdf (site discontinued).

38   Department of Human Services, Australian Government, *New South Wales Bushfires: October 2013*. Available at: www.humanservices.gov.au/customer/services/centrelink/dra-nsw-bushfires-october-2013 (site discontinued).

39   Department of Human Services, Australian Government, *Western Australia Bushfires: January 2014*. Available at: www.humanservices.gov.au/customer/enablers/centrelink/australian-government-disaster-recovery-payment/western-australia-bushfires-january-2014 (site discontinued).

40   See for example Department of Human Services, Australian Government, *Ex-Gratia Income Support Allowance for New Zealand Non-Protected Special Category Visa Holders: NSW Bushfires October 2013*. Available at: www.humanservices.gov.au/customer/enablers/centrelink/disaster-recovery-allowance/ex-gratia-income-support-allowance-nsw-bushfires-oct-2013#a4 (site discontinued).

diplomatically unpalatable, the federal government feels compelled to repeatedly patch the system by applying the band-aid of ex-gratia payments.

Another anomaly affecting New Zealanders who have settled in Australia after 2001 is that they will be required to contribute to the National Disability Insurance Scheme — now called Disability Care Australia — but will not be entitled to access any of the support it provides. This is because the residency requirements for eligibility under the *National Disability Insurance Scheme Act 2013* (Cth) exclude New Zealanders who are not protected SCV holders.[41] However, the definition of 'Australian resident' in the *Health Insurance Act 1973* makes all SCV holders (protected and unprotected alike) liable to pay the Medicare levy and the additional impost to finance the disability scheme.[42] As a result, 'many New Zealand citizens will be directly taxed for a disability scheme they cannot access'.[43] It is hard not to sympathise with the view that this amounts to unfair and discriminatory treatment.

In many states it is already the case that New Zealanders are ineligible for support services if they live with a disability. When cerebral palsy sufferer Hannah Campbell challenged her treatment in court, the Queensland Government agreed to pay an undisclosed sum to cover the costs of her care. However, because the matter was settled out of court, the case failed to set a precedent for other New Zealanders. As her lawyer commented at the time, the Queensland Government dodged a 'multimillion-dollar bullet'.[44] The introduction of Disability Care Australia will eliminate the differences between states and remove any doubt — New Zealanders will be excluded from support services.[45]

---

41 *National Disability Insurance Scheme Act 2013* (Cth) ch 3 pt 123.

42 *Health Insurance Act 1973* (Cth) pt 1 s 3(1)c.

43 David Faulkner, above fn 17.

44 Ben Heather, Kiwis' Australian Care Case Settled', *Stuff NZ*, 25 October 2012. Available at: www.stuff.co.nz/world/australia/7858803/Kiwis-Australian-care-case-settled.

45 The set of government entitlements available or denied to non-protected SCV holders is complicated and varies between different states and territories. For example, New Zealand tertiary students receive concessional public transport fares in New South Wales but not in Victoria. For further discussion of this issue see Peter Mares, 'A Special Category' (2014) 43 *Griffith Review*. Available at: griffithreview.com/articles/9677/; David Faulkner, above fn 17.

It might be objected that New Zealanders who have been living and working in Australia on non-protected SCVs could obviate all these problems by becoming Australian residents. Often, however, this is not a straightforward matter. In accord with the 1973 bilateral Trans-Tasman Travel Arrangement, all New Zealanders are granted an SCV on arrival in Australia (unless there are health or character concerns).[46] There are no qualification requirements for New Zealanders to enter the Australian workforce, and although the *Migration Act 1958* (Cth) describes the visa as a 'temporary visa',[47] there are no limits on the duration of stay. However, a New Zealander who aspires to become a permanent resident of Australia must meet the same occupational, health, and age requirements as any other applicant in the skilled or family streams of the migration program. If New Zealanders are not the immediate family member of an Australian citizen, or if they do not have a profession that is in short supply — such as a profession on the Consolidated Sponsored Occupation List[48] — or if they are over 50 years of age, then it is unlikely that they will ever qualify for permanent residency. The amount of time they have spent living and working in Australia is of marginal benefit to their migration application but never sufficient to secure permanent residency without satisfying other criteria.

Example 4: Childhood immunisation

Another example of the way in which regulatory systems fail to adequately account for the increase in long-term temporary migration to Australia is childhood immunisation. In the interests of public health, the Australian Government provides free childhood vaccinations for a wide range of communicable diseases, however, this service is restricted to citizens, permanent residents, and other people eligible to hold a Medicare card (so in this case all New Zealanders do qualify).[49]

---

46   *Migration Act 1958* (Cth) pt 2 div 3 sub-div A s32.
47   Ibid.
48   An occupation on this list is required for permanent migration under the skills stream via employer or a state or territory government nomination.
49   See, for example, Department of Health, Victorian Government, *Free Vaccine Victoria – Criteria For Eligibility*. Available at: www.health.vic.gov.au/immunisation/free-vaccine.htm (site discontinued). The Commonwealth Department of Health confirms that the same eligibility criteria apply nationwide (email correspondence with the author, 13 October 2013).

According to a community nurse and midwife working in Victoria, public health staff in her local government area have been instructed to tell 457 visa holders, international students, and other temporary visa holders who are not eligible for free immunisations that they should take their baby or child to a general practitioner for vaccination.[50] While international students and 457 visa holders are required to take out private health insurance that may rebate the cost of vaccinations (at least up to the level of the standard Medicare rebate), she is concerned that this restriction may result in immunisations being postponed or not carried out at all. Migrants and culturally and linguistically diverse communities are regarded as one of the 'special-risk and under-served populations' for immunisation.[51] As a result, tracking the percentage of children who are fully immunised is more difficult in areas with large immigrant populations.[52] While immunisation providers are expected to have a comprehensive understanding of the eligibility rules for access to free or subsidised vaccines, 'differences in eligibility by vaccine and visa class add complexity and act as a barrier to the provision of catch-up immunisation' in communities that are 'particularly vulnerable to under-immunisation'.[53] Excluding a proportion of that migration population from mass immunisation schemes on the basis of their visa status serves to further complicate an already complex situation. Given official concern at gaps in comprehensive childhood immunisation in Australia,[54] this policy appears decidedly short-sighted.

50   Personal interview with the author (15 November 2013). Name withheld at interviewee's request for privacy reasons.

51   National Centre for Immunisation Research and Surveillance, 'Biennial Report: January 2010 – November 2011' (2012). Available at: www.ncirs.edu.au/assets/publications/reports/NCIRS-biennial-report-2010-2011.pdf.

52   The National Health Performance Authority, *Healthy Communities: Immunization Rates for Children in 2012–13*. Available at: www.myhealthycommunities.gov.au/Content/publications/downloads/NHPA_HC_Report_Imm_Rates_March_2014.pdf.

53   NHMRC Centre for Research Excellence in Population Health, *Protecting Australia: Closing the Gap in Immunisation for Migrants and Refugees: Proceedings from a Stakeholder Workshop*. Available at: creimmunisation.com.au/sites/default/files/newsevents/events/Proceedings_CRE MigrantRefugeeWorkshop.pdf.

54   See, for example, The National Health Performance Authority, 'Childhood Immunisation Rates Up, But Some Areas Still Low', (Media Release, 24 March 2014).

The rise and rise of temporary migration

Temporary migration is no longer some marginal or temporary phenomenon at the edges of our migration program, but is now central to it. Increasingly, Australia has a 'two step' or 'try before you buy' migration program, which means a growing share of people taking up places in Australia's permanent migration program are already living here and have often been living here for several years.

The increase in temporary migration to Australia since 1999 is illustrated in Figure 4.1. For reasons outlined below, the number of 485 (skilled graduate) visa holders — the smallest category shown — can be expected to increase sharply in coming years.

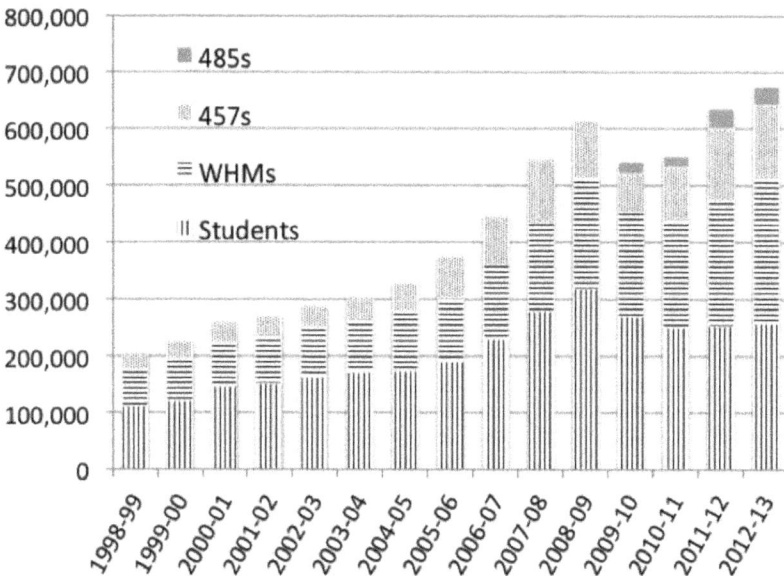

Figure 4.1: Growth in temporary visas issued 1999–2013.

Note: Includes both primary and secondary visa holders. WHM includes both 'Working Holiday Maker' visas and 'Work and Holiday Maker' visas.

Source: Department of Immigration and Citizenship.[55]

---

55   The department has since been renamed the Department of Immigration and Border Protection, and has been known by other names in previous years (such as the Department of Immigration and Multicultural Affairs). Specific source documents are 'Annual Report' (1999–2013); 'Student Visa Program' (2006–07 to 2012–13); 'Subclass 457 State/Territory Summary Report' (2007–13), 'Working Holiday Maker Visa Program Report' (30 June 2013); 'Working Holiday and Work and Holiday Visa Report', 2005–06 to 2009–10 Program Years.

The substantial contribution of New Zealanders to Net Overseas Migration (NOM) to Australia is shown in Figure 4.2. As a result of the 2001 changes to the definition of 'Australian resident' outlined above, a growing proportion of Australia's New Zealand-born population are denied substantial entitlements that accrue to permanent residents.

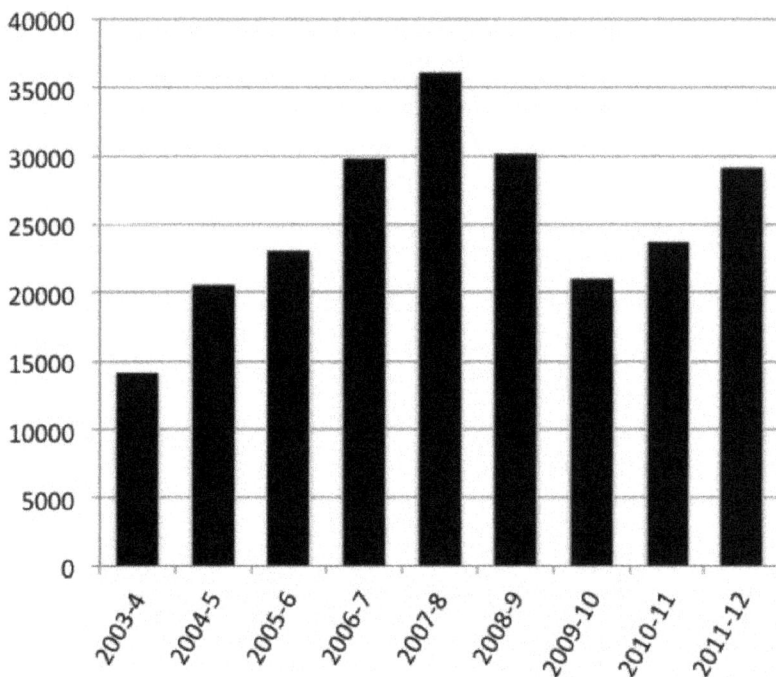

Figure 4.2: New Zealand contribution to Net Overseas Migration 2004–12.
Source: Department of Immigration and Citizenship.[56]

The number of temporary skilled migrants entering Australia each year under the 457 visa program now rivals (and sometimes exceeds) the size of the annual permanent skilled migration intake, as shown in Figure 4.3.

---

56   Department of Immigration and Citizenship, 'Australian Migration Trends 2011–12' (2012) 98.

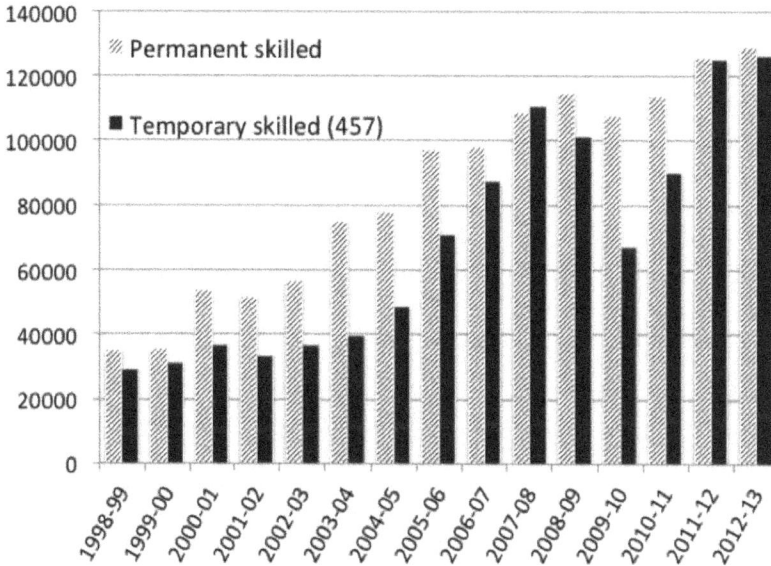

Figure 4.3: Temporary v permanent skilled visas 1999–2013.
Source: Department of Immigration and Citizenship.[57]

Another indication of the growing importance of temporary migration to Australia can be seen in the number of temporary migrants present in Australia at any given time. In the seven years from 2006 to 2013, the number more than doubled, from around 350,000 temporary migrants to close to 800,000. It should be noted, too, that in addition to the four categories of visa holders depicted in Figure 4.4 (457 visa holders, 485 visa holders, bridging visa holders, and working holiday makers), by 2013 there were an estimated 200,000 New Zealanders living in Australia on non-protected SCVs.[58] As outlined above, despite their right to reside and work in Australia indefinitely, in many respects this cohort of New Zealanders are in a similar situation to temporary migrants.

---

57   Department of Immigration and Citizenship, 'Annual Report' (1999–2013); 'Subclass 457 State/Territory Summary Report' (2007–13).
58   Kate McMillan and Paul Harmer, 'Kiwis in Australia Deserve Better', *New Zealand Herald*, 10 October 2013. Available at: www.nzherald.co.nz/nz/news/article.cfm?c_id=1& objectid=11137557.

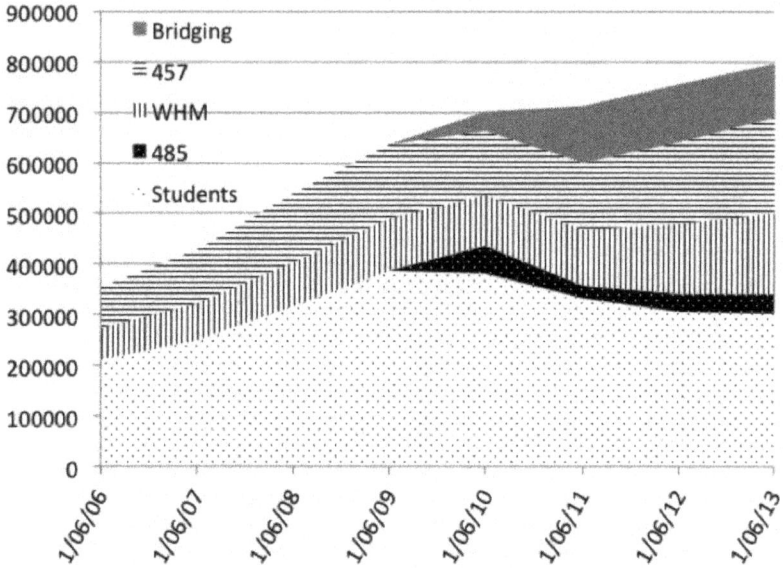

Figure 4.4: Temporary residents with work rights 2006–13 (stock).
Source: Department of Immigration and Citizenship.[59]

As shown in Figure 4.5, temporary migrants with work rights make up a significant and growing proportion of the Australian labour force, with the share rising from 3.3 per cent in 2006 to 6.4 per cent in 2013. (This calculation excludes New Zealanders on non-protected SCVs. Their inclusion would take the share closer to 9 per cent.)

---

59   Immigration Updates 2006–10, Temporary Entrants and NZ Citizens in Australia Quarterly Reports 2011–13. It might be argued that bridging visa holders should not be included in this calculation, however, most bridging visa holders do have work rights. The growth in the number of bridging visa holders is in itself evidence of the growing gap between the demand and supply of permanent residency spots, since many bridging visa holders are stuck in the processing 'queue' for residency.

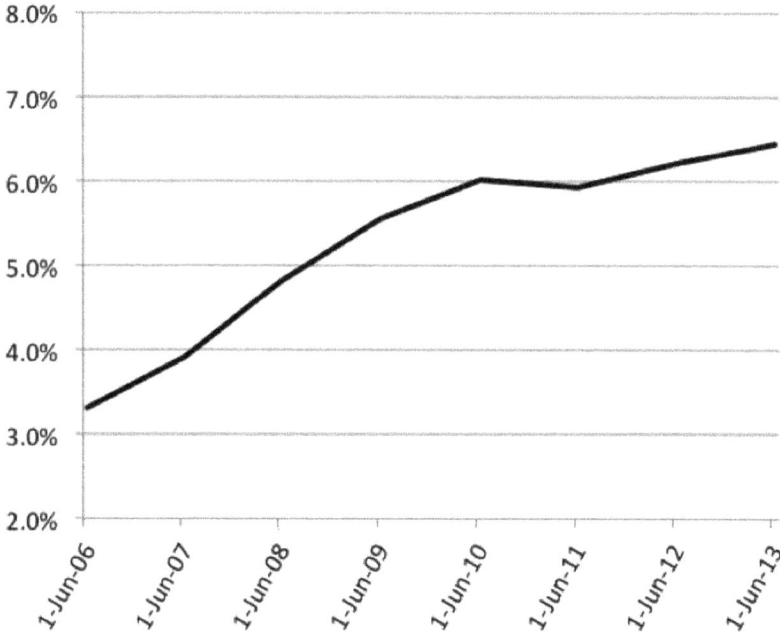

Figure 4.5: Temporary residents as percentage of the labour force.
Source: Department of Immigration and Citizenship and Australian Bureau of Statistics.[60]

Implications

In considering the rapid growth in temporary migration to Australia in recent years, two facts are particularly important.

Firstly, the permanent migration program has an annual cap, while the number of temporary migrants admitted to the country is open-ended. Secondly, a significant proportion of temporary migrants hope to settle permanently in Australia. The most comprehensive available survey of 457 (temporary skilled worker) visa holders, for example, suggests that around 70 per cent intend to apply for permanent residency when their temporary visa expires,[61] while a 2007 survey of international students found 65 per cent intended to seek permanent

---

60   Ibid., and Australian Bureau of Statistics, *Series 6202 Labour Force, Australia*. Available at: www.abs.gov.au/ausstats/abs%40.nsf/mf/6202.0. If the estimated 200,000 New Zealanders on non-protected SCVs was included, the proportion would be more than 8 per cent.
61   Scott Morrison, above fn 5.

residency.[62] (One survey of second-year accounting students at a Melbourne University found that 84 per cent intended to seek permanent residency.)[63]

Given these two facts, it appears likely that, over time, Australia will experience an increasing mismatch between the aspirations of temporary migrants to become permanent residents and the capacity of growing numbers of them to realise that goal.

Already the data shows a growing gap between the number of 457 visas issued each year and the number of 457 visa holders who convert to permanent residency. As can be seen in Figure 4.6, the number of 457 visas converting annually to permanent residency has stagnated since 2008–09, despite a large increase in the number of temporary visas issued in subsequent years.

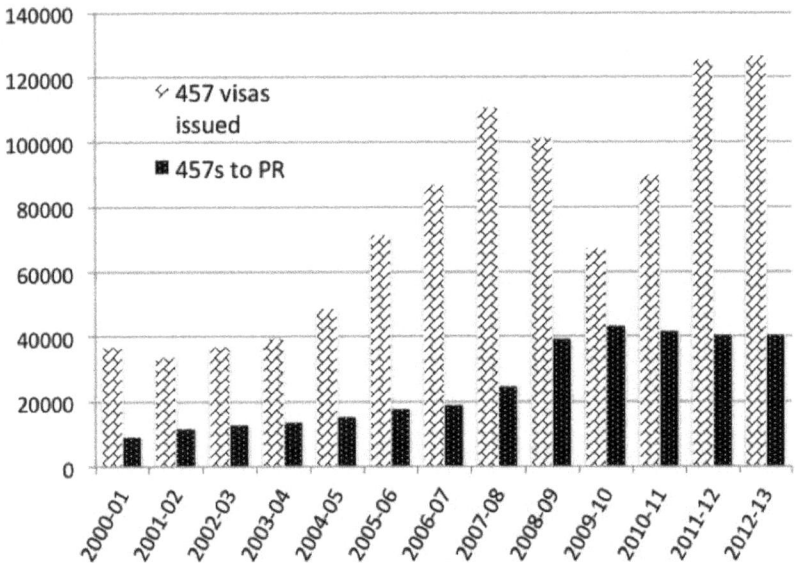

Figure 4.6: Conversion of 457 visas to permanent residency.
Source: Department of Immigration and Citizenship.[64]

---

62   Cindy Tilbrook, 'International Students: Perspectives and Graduate Outcomes' (Australian International Education Conference, 2007).
63   Beverly Jackling, 'The Lure of Permanent Residency and the Aspirations and Expectations of International Students Studying Accounting in Australia' (2007) 15 *People and Place* 31.
64   Department of Immigration and Citizenship, 'Annual Report' (2000–13); Department of Immigration and Citizenship, 'Subclass 457 State/Territory Summary Report' (2007–13).

We can anticipate that this gap will grow larger as the demand for permanent places continues to outstrip the supply, especially given that 457 visa holders are only one category of temporary migrants seeking to convert to permanent residency. As Robertson noted in the previous chapter, 'longer-term migration' seems to be a 'core focus' of many of the migrants on relatively short-term working holiday (417) and post-study work (485) visas.

This is likely to generate a growing cohort of temporary migrants who continue living in Australia for extended periods of time on a series of temporary visas, either by repeatedly renewing an existing work visa (such as a 457 visa) or by switching between different visa categories (moving from student visa to 457 visa, for example).

The numbers involved are potentially large.

Of the 81,547 primary applications for a subclass 457 visa lodged in 2012–13, the majority (42,610 or 52 per cent) were lodged onshore — that is, they were lodged by people who were already present in Australia as temporary migrants.[65]

Similarly, in the 2012–13 financial year, approximately 53,000 international student graduates extended their stay in Australia by switching to a different temporary visa category with work rights — 32,000 moved onto a 485 temporary graduate work visa; 18,000 moved onto a temporary skilled 457 visa; and 3,000 moved onto a working holiday maker visa.[66] This was more than three times the number of student graduates that moved onto a *permanent* skilled visa.[67] A further 30,000 students shifted from one type of student visa to another — from vocational education to university education, for example.[68]

---

65   Department of Immigration and Border Protection, answer to question taken on notice, (AE14/217) Additional Estimates, Australian Senate, 25 February 2014.
66   Department of Immigration and Citizenship, 'Student Visa Program Quarterly Report Quarter Ending at 30 June 2013' (2013). The largest categories of visa holders applying onshore for 457 visas were existing 457 visa holders, international students and student graduates and working holiday makers. Only a small number of tourists were included.
67   Ibid.
68   Ibid.

The number of student graduates transitioning to a 485 temporary graduate visa can be expected to grow substantially in coming years, because changes to the scheme introduced in March 2013 make it much easier for international students to remain living and working in Australia after completing their studies.[69] The changes extend the visa's duration from 18 months to two years work visa if a student has studied in Australia for at least 16 months and completed either a bachelor's degree or a master's degree by course work. Students who complete a master's by research can qualify for a three-year visa, while those who complete a doctorate get four years.

Applicants do not need to be qualified for one of the jobs on the Skilled Occupation List (an official list of job categories deemed to be in short supply in the Australian economy), nor is there any requirement that they work in the professional field in which they qualified. Any graduate who is under 50 years of age and has competent English is eligible for a 485 visa as long as their first visa to study in Australia was granted on or after 5 November 2011.[70]

The visa changes were driven by a desire to make Australian universities more attractive to full-fee paying overseas students. A review of Australia's international education industry declared in 2011 that 'the absence of clearly defined post-study work rights entitlement puts Australian universities at a very serious disadvantage compared to some of our major competitor countries', and concluded that an expanded work visa was essential to 'the ongoing viability of our universities in an increasingly competitive global market for students'.[71]

With the introduction of the revamped 485 visa, it is now entirely conceivable that a student might arrive in Australia at the age of 16 to complete the final two years of high school, then go on to do a three-year undergraduate degree, a year of honours, and a two-year master's as an international student before working for three years

---

69   *Migration Regulations 1994* (Cth); *Migration Legislation Amendment Regulation* (No 1) 2013 (Cth) sch 2. See also Peter Mares, 'We Know About the 457. What About the 485?' *Inside Story*, 28 March 2013. Available at: inside.org.au/we-know-about-the-457-what-about-the-485/.

70   Department of Immigration and Border Protection, *Temporary Graduate Visa (subclass 485)*. Available at: www.immi.gov.au/Visas/Pages/485.aspx (site discontinued).

71   Michael Knight, 'Strategic Review of the Student Visa Program 2011' (Report to the Australian Government, June 2011) viii.

on a 485 graduate visa. At the end of this period, the student will be aged 27 and will have spent 11 formative years in Australia. He or she will have invested tens if not hundreds of thousands of dollars on fees for education, and will very likely have paid a significant amount of tax, but will not necessarily be on a pathway to becoming an Australian resident and enjoying the rights and entitlements that go with permanent residency or citizenship.

Ethical and practical problems

What should be our ethical response to the rise of temporary migration and how should this inform policy?

We might argue, together with Michael Walzer, that all temporary labour migration should cease because it is morally objectionable and renders the nation equivalent to 'a family with live-in servants'.[72] Walzer would argue that if we decide as a nation that we need to import more workers, then we should be willing to enlarge our political community to include them as citizens.

Given the spread of temporary migration programs, not just in Australia but globally, bolting horses and stable doors come to mind in response to this argument. It also fails to deal with the complexity of cross border movements — how would you apply it to international students who come to Australia initially for education, who may also work while they are here, and who intend to return to their home country, even though this intention may (and often does) change?[73]

Joo-Cheong Tham has approached the ethical challenge posed by temporary migration in a different way, by asking how we reconcile temporary migration with our conception of justice. He identifies four different responses to this question.[74] The first is to argue that justice is irrelevant. The line of argument here makes reference to Australian Prime Minister John Howard's statement in response to the *Tampa* affair that 'we' (that is, sovereign governments) 'will decide

---

72   Michael Walzer, above fn 16, 52.
73   Shanthi Robertson, above fn 11, 24.
74   Joo-Cheong Tham, 'Multiculturalism and Temporary Migration: Where Does Justice Fit?' (Presentation to Australian Multicultural Commission roundtable, Melbourne, 15 March 2013).

who comes to this country and the circumstances under which they come'.[75] Under this view, justice for temporary migrants is entirely at the discretion of the host government.

A second argument is that in questions of justice, citizens get priority. Under this view, the rights of temporary migrants exist, but in any conflict will always be trumped by the rights of citizens. We can see this view reflected in the comments of former Prime Minister Julia Gillard that she wanted 'to stop foreign workers being put at the front of the queue with Australian workers at the back'.[76] We might have some sympathy for this view, but question how far it should go. Does it mean, as some unions have argued for example, that in the case of redundancies, temporary migrant workers should always be sacked first? This is dangerous territory, because it grants employers arbitrary power over a particular group of workers that could result in exploitation.

As Tham says, '[i]t is one thing to design immigration admission criteria administered by government departments' to give priority to the employment of citizens and permanent residents, but another to do this 'through private sector actors'.[77]

The third approach identified by Tham is 'justice based on choice'. Under this view, temporary migrants have implicitly accepted the rules of the game by deciding to come to Australia in the first place. They have chosen to make their beds in Australia, and they should lie in them, without complaint.

But this 'take it or leave it' approach runs contrary to our understanding of Australia as a nation based on liberal democratic values, 'principles that organise — and encourage — engagement, debate and disagreement in the political process'.[78] This approach also ignores the impact of time, and the way in which duration of stay not only gives rise to a sense of belonging on the side of the migrant, but also to ethical obligations on the part of the recipient state. As Carens argues:

---

75   John Howard, Speech at the Federal Liberal Party Campaign Launch (28 October 2001).

76   *The Economist*, 'Winning the West', 16 March 2013. Available at: www.economist.com/news/asia/21573609-prime-minister-canvasses-fast-changing-suburbs-winning-west.

77   Joo-Cheong Tham, above fn 74.

78   Ibid.

The ties that come from actually living in a state are the most powerful basis for a claim to membership. Home is where one lives, and where one lives is the crucial variable for interests and for identity, both empirically and normatively.[79]

Tham's fourth — and preferred — approach to the question of justice for temporary migrants is justice as fairness. This does not mean identical treatment for everyone — whether citizen, permanent resident, or temporary migrant — but it does mean bringing the concept of fairness into play when considering the rights and entitlements of long-term temporary migrants who are making a significant contribution to the economic, social, and cultural life of the nation.

Introducing notions of fairness into the discussion does not automatically solve practical policy questions, but it does at least change the nature of the debate because it forces us to conceptualise long-term temporary migrants as human beings, rather than as '"pure" economic inputs' who can be expected to simply depart when their labour is no longer required or their tuition fees have been expended.[80]

Applying the lens of fairness can help us to respond to the case studies outlined above, although it does not obviate the need to make normative judgements that will be open to contestation. As Carens notes, 'the extremes will be clear, the middle will be fuzzy'.[81]

Let us begin with the case of Claire Hewitt. The premise of fairness would require that a temporary migrant worker be entitled to the same workplace rights and entitlement as an employee who is an Australian citizen or permanent resident. This is the conclusion reached by Carens, who argues that 'minimum acceptable working conditions' are based on 'the understanding of what is acceptable that is generated by the community's internal democratic processes'.[82] On this basis, the state should regulate working conditions in the same way for citizens, residents, and temporary migrants.[83]

---

79 Joseph Carens, *The Ethics of Immigration* (Oxford University Press, 2013) 31.
80 Catherine Dauvergne and Sarah Marsden, above fn 6.
81 Joseph H Carens, above fn 8, 435.
82 Ibid., 426.
83 One potential exception to this principle is labour mobility — that is, whether a temporary migrant is tied to a particular employer or is at liberty to change jobs. This issue is discussed further below, in the context of economic and social rights.

Indeed, this appears to be the foundation of present policy in Australia, which requires potential employers to show that they will provide 'no less favourable terms and conditions of employment' to a 457 visa holder 'than they would to an equivalent Australian in the sponsor's workplace at the same location'.[84] Further, 457 visa holders are entitled to the same 'basic rights and protections in the workplace'[85] as Australian employees, including 'the right not to be dismissed unfairly' and 'the right to join and be represented by a trade union'.[86]

If we apply this logic to the case of Claire Hewitt, then the fair course of action becomes apparent. Given that her accident was a workplace accident, she should be treated no differently to a citizen or permanent resident in the same situation. The intent of the *Workers Rehabilitation and Compensation Act* (NT) should be honoured. If giving full effect to the meaning of rehabilitation under the Act requires that Claire Hewitt be granted permanent residency, then that is what should happen (and the legislation of this and other comparable Acts around Australia should be amended accordingly to ensure that temporary migrant workers affected by workplace accidents are treated on equal terms with their Australian colleagues).[87]

If we apply the same principles of fairness and equality in workplace rights and entitlements to the second case study of international students formerly employed by the collapsed Swan Services Cleaning Group, then we will reach a similar conclusion. The eligibility definitions in the *Fair Entitlements Guarantee Act 2012* (Cth) should be amended to extend coverage to temporary migrants with work rights, such as international students and 457 visa holders.

The issues involved in case studies three and four are potentially more complex, since they raise questions about access to government services. These are rights and entitlements that do not emanate from an employment relationship in the workplace but from physical

---

84   Department of Immigration and Border Protection, 'Temporary Work (Skilled) (subclass 457) Visa Information Booklet'. Available at: www.immi.gov.au/allforms/booklets/books9.pdf (site discontinued).

85   Ibid., 47.

86   Ibid., 48.

87   An alternative way of looking at Hewitt's case would be to regard workplace injury compensation as a contributory insurance scheme, albeit with the employer, rather than the employee, paying the premiums. But even if we take this approach, the 'fair' outcome would be the same, for reasons discussed below.

presence within the boundaries of a political community. Questions of fairness thus run in two directions: is it fair that citizens and permanent residents should contribute via taxation to the welfare of migrants whose stay in Australia may only be temporary and whose contribution to government revenue may be limited as a result?

This returns us to the puzzling problem identified by Carens:

> What are the claims of non-citizens who are present on the territory of a state but who are not permanent residents? Does the normative map of democracy have room for them?[88]

Taken narrowly, the issues of access to emergency disaster relief, disability care, and childhood immunisation can be seen as questions of entitlement to government-funded services and welfare. As we shall see, however, digging around in such particular issues soon raises the broader question of political belonging and whether, as Carens argues, the passage of time means that a 'temporary visa ... ought at some point to be converted into a right of permanent residence'.[89]

Let us restrict our gaze for now to the question of government services.

In this context, Martin Ruhs distinguishes between 'contributory' and 'means-tested' entitlements.[90] Carens makes a similar distinction between 'social programs directly tied to workforce participation' (such as unemployment insurance and compulsory retirement savings schemes) and 'other social programs', which might include healthcare, education, low income tax credits, 'and anything else the state spends money on for the benefit of the domestic population'.[91]

If we follow Carens and Ruhs, temporary migrants should be entitled to benefits under the former category, but not necessarily under the latter. In an Australian context, compulsory superannuation payments would be an example of a 'contributory' entitlement and it is uncontroversial that migrant workers retain ownership of their accumulated funds.

---

88   Joseph H Carens, above fn 8, 420.

89   Ibid., 422.

90   Martin Ruhs, *The Price of Rights: Regulating International Labour Migration* (Princeton University Press, 2013) 189.

91   Joseph H Carens, above fn 8, 425.

Most government services in Australia are funded through general taxation revenue, however, and would fall into the latter category, although the situation is not straightforward. Healthcare and school education in Australia are universal and not means-tested. They are not 'contributory' or 'directly tied to workplace participation' as such, but in the case of Medicare, the costs are partly recovered through a specific levy on income. This is also true of the National Disability Insurance Scheme.

Most government-funded or subsidised services are automatically available regardless of an individual's visa status. You do not need to prove residency to use public transport or call on the help of police or the fire brigade. Carens argues that fundamental entitlements like healthcare and school education should also be treated in this manner:

> … any state that treats health care as a basic right … is obliged to provide health care to temporary workers, and their families, too, if they are present. Every democratic state has a system of free and compulsory public education, and again, temporary workers have a right to this education for their children if their children are present.[92]

Carens also argues that:

> It is blatantly unfair to require people to pay into an insurance scheme if they are not eligible for the benefits. This violates an elementary principle of reciprocity.[93]

Applying Carens' logic would require New Zealanders on SCVs to be included in the National Disability Insurance Scheme, potentially after some qualification period linked to the duration of their residency. It would also require that the children of long-term temporary migrants be provided with free immunisation, and would also entitle those children to free education (which 457 visa holders are entitled to in some states but not in others).

Carens also provides the basis for arguing for a change of policy such that all long-term temporary migrants would be eligible for services under Medicare and the National Disability Insurance Scheme, if they

---

92   Ibid., 429.
93   Ibid., 426.

pay the appropriate levies, and again, after an appropriate qualification period linked to the amount of time they have spent living, working, and paying tax in Australia.

But what might an appropriate qualification period be? This is also the question that confronts us in relation to disaster relief and after what period long-term temporary migrants, such as New Zealander SCV holders, should be entitled to emergency payments during events such as floods and bushfires. In other words, it brings us back to the Carens core question of political belonging.

As Dauvergne and Marsden point out, expanding the 'rights' of temporary migrants can bring them tangible benefits, but can only go so far before running up against its inherent limitation:

> It is impossible … within rights discourse, to erase the underlying subordination of temporary migrant workers. Talking in rights terms, inevitably calls up the 'right' of the state to exclude non-members as an aspect of sovereignty. This exclusion power undermines attempts to articulate rights claims for those with any type of temporary status, and reinforces a fundamental inequality between citizens and non-citizens.[94]

Ruhs identifies the same problem in a different way, when he argues that there should be no restrictions on the fundamental civil and political rights of temporary migrant workers — such as freedom of thought and expression, freedom of religious belief and worship, and freedom of association — with the crucial exception of the right to vote in national elections and the right to run for public office.[95] These are two rights that usually demarcate the boundaries of citizenship.

As long as migrants remain temporary, they remain outside that boundary. And while Ruhs accepts restrictions on certain social and economic rights of temporary migrants — not just government benefits but also the right to family reunion and freedom of movement within the labour market — his caveat is that any such restrictions

---

94   Catherine Dauvergne and Sarah Marsden, above fn 6, 237.
95   Martin Ruhs, above fn 91, 187.

must be time limited. He argues, following Carens, that 'the passage of time' is 'the most important consideration' in strengthening migrants' 'moral claims'.[96]

Ruhs thus concludes that there should be a point at which temporary migrants are either granted permanent residence or required to return home. He rejects potential outcomes in which migrants repeatedly renew time-limited visas or cycle through different categories of temporary visas, as can potentially happen in Australia today. If restrictions on migrants' social and economic rights are not time-limited, he argues, then we risk creating a group of 'second-class residents' — residents who are not only at risk of being permanently temporary, but are also at risk of being permanently excluded from the political community of the nation, and permanently denied the benefits and rights of citizenship.[97]

What should this time limit be? Ruhs considers four years — equivalent to a single term on a 457 visa — to be a reasonable period, though he offers little justification for choosing this number beyond gut feeling — less than three years seems too short and more than five years seems too long.[98]

In her review of the integrity of the 457 visa system, Industrial Relations Commissioner Barbara Deegan reached a similar conclusion to Ruhs on the indefinite and repeated renewal of temporary work permits, recommending that no 457 visa holder 'be permitted to remain in Australia for more than 8 years in total'.[99] If they were unable to convert to permanent residency after that time, she recommended that they be required to leave Australia.

In Australia, we have established other time thresholds in relation to migration. For example, a permanent resident must wait two years to become eligible for most social security payments,[100] and a permanent resident must satisfy a four-year residency requirement

---

96   Joseph H Carens, *Immigrants and the Right to Stay* (MIT Press, 2010) 6. (Carens was referring here to irregular migrants but the same principle is applicable to temporary migrants.)

97   Martin Ruhs, above fn 91, 191.

98   Ibid., 192.

99   Barbara Deegan, above fn 2.

100 Department of Human Services, Australian Government, *Newly Arrived Resident's Waiting Period*. Available at: www.humanservices.gov.au/customer/enablers/newly-arrived-residents-waiting-period.

before applying for citizenship.[101] There is a 10-year time frame after which a child born in Australia to non-citizen or non-resident parents gains the right to citizenship.[102] Another 10-year time frame applies to limited access to certain government benefits for New Zealanders on non-protected SCVs.[103]

There is a proposal to introduce a similar 10-year residency threshold to enable New Zealand SCV holders who arrived in Australia as children to gain access to the Higher Education Contribution Scheme/Higher Education Loan Programme loans scheme to attend university or TAFE.[104] (Currently they must pay upfront fees.)

If we were to apply Ruhs' approach of gut feeling to this issue, then 10 years would appear a very long qualification period. By comparison, Carens notes a European Union directive that recommends that 'third country nationals (that is, people from outside the EU) be granted a right of permanent residence if they have been legally residing in a single EU state for five years'.[105] Time spent in the country as a student is discounted by 50 per cent as long as the applicant has held another temporary resident status in addition to student status.[106] In Canada, a temporary migration scheme for live-in caregivers leads to permanent residency after two years full-time employment.[107]

The point of such examples is not to suggest that there is an objectively identifiable or average time period at which temporary migration should transition to permanent residence (or before which long-

---

101 *Australian Citizenship Act 2007* (Cth) pt 2 div 1 s 22.
102 Ibid., pt 2 div 1 s 12(b).
103 If you arrived in Australia on a New Zealand passport and have lived here for at least 10 continuous years since 26 February 2001, you may be able to access a once-only payment of Newstart Allowance, Sickness Allowance, or Youth Allowance. If you are eligible, payment can be made for a maximum continuous period of up to six months. See Department of Human Services, Australian Government, *New Zealand Citizens Claiming Payments in Australia.* Available at: www.humanservices.gov.au/customer/enablers/nz-citizens-claiming-payments-in-australia.
104 Radio New Zealand News, *Some Kiwi Students to Get Australian Loans.* Available at: www.radionz.co.nz/news/political/235456/some-kiwi-students-to-get-australian-loans.
105 Joseph H Carens, above fn 8, 419. The directive in question is European Council Directive 2003/109/EC.
106 Shanthi Robertson, above fn 11, 38. This means, for example, that a combination of four years study and three years work would render a temporary migrant eligible.
107 Citizenship and Immigration Canada, *Become a Permanent Resident: Live-in Caregivers* (19 October 2012). Available at: www.cic.gc.ca/english/work/caregiver/permanent_resident.asp.

term temporary migration should be curtailed and migrants forced to leave). Rather, it is to agree with Carens that 'some threshold must be established beyond which the right to stay is indefeasible'.[108]

As with the time thresholds described above, there will, inevitably, be an element of arbitrariness as to where the limit is set:

> Why five years rather than four or six? No one can pretend that the answer to this question entails any fundamental principle. It is more a matter of the social psychology of coordination, given the need to settle on one point within a range. But if one asks why five years rather than one or ten, it is easier to make the case that one is too short and ten too long, given common European understandings of the ways in which people settle into the societies where they live.[109]

Accepting the need for some limit presupposes accepting Carens' argument that 'the longer one stays in a society, the stronger one's claim to remain'.[110] But this appears to be a widely accepted common sense understanding. As former immigration minister Scott Morrison acknowledged (whilst still in Opposition):

> When we arrive in this country, we become part of it — and it becomes a part of us — it becomes what [Sir Henry] Parkes described as 'the land of our adoption'. It changes us — and in doing so it provides the basis for our connection with one another.[111]

Migrants who live in Australia for a significant period of time, who contribute to the economic life of the nation through their labour and their taxes, and who possibly pay fees to study, are people who, for all intents and purposes, make Australia their home.

Should we, as Ruhs and Deegan suggest, force people to leave before that connection becomes too strong — that is, before their emotional, psychological, financial, and cultural bonds to Australia reach the point at which 'a threshold is crossed, and they acquire a moral claim to have their actual social membership legally recognised'?[112] If so, should the time limit be four years, or five, or six, or 10? Is it also

---

108 Joseph H Carens, above fn 8, 422.
109 Ibid.
110 Ibid.
111 Scott Morrison, 'Reasons to Be Optimistic about Australia's Immigration Future' (Address to the Affinity Intercultural Foundation, Sydney, 17 July 2013).
112 Joseph H Carens, *Immigrants and the Right to Stay*, above fn 97, 18.

plausible that the moral claim that increases with duration of stay might be linked to the age and life stage of the person in question? Does it make a difference, for example, if a 24-year-old has spent eight years — a third of his or her life — living in Australia since the age of 16, compared to a 48-year-old who arrived at age 40 and who has spent only one-sixth of his or her life here? Should a point come at which continuous residency automatically confers the right of permanency? Such an option may have its own unintended consequences.[113] Is there a middle way, in which each year of temporary residence increases an applicant's points in an application for permanent residency, perhaps with time spent as a student discounted as compared to time spent as an employee?

As Australia's system of temporary migration continues to expand, it moves us further away from the postwar certainties of settler migration. Yet, as Robertson notes, 'countries like Australia are, conceptually and politically, largely unprepared for the consequences of increased temporary migration schemes',[114] (intended and unintended). We talk about temporary migration quite a lot in Australia, but debate still tends to be limited to the specifics of rights and entitlements. For example, we question whether international students qualify for public transport discounts, or whether 457 visa holders should pay for their children to attend state schools. Similarly, we debate issues of enforcement and protection — how do we ensure that temporary migrant workers are not exploited at work? These are legitimate and important matters, but as I have argued above, they lead ultimately to the larger threshold question of political membership: at what point does, or should, 'temporary' become 'permanent'? There is no simple answer to this question, and any answer will be contested. It is a matter that can only be resolved politically, and a political response can only be generated through robust debate. Currently, however, we generally fail to pose the question at all.

---

113 For example, there have been cases in which undocumented migrants have sought to extend their stay in Australia in order for an Australian-born child to cross the 10-year threshold required for citizenship. See Peter Mares, 'A Routine Removal' (2007) 18 *Griffith Review* 205.
114 Shanthi Robertson, above fn 11, 167.

Bibliography

Articles, books, and reports

Carens, Joseph H, 'Live-in Domestics, Seasonal Workers, and Others Hard to Locate on the Map of Democracy' (2008) 16 *The Journal of Political Philosophy* 419

Carens, Joseph H, *Immigrants and the Right to Stay* (MIT Press, 2010)

Carens, Joseph H, *The Ethics of Immigration* (Oxford University Press, 2013)

Dauvergne, Barbara and Sarah Marsden, 'The Ideology of Temporary Labour Migration in the Post-Global Era' (2014) 18 *Citizenship Studies* 224

Deegan, Barbara, 'Visa Subclass 457 Integrity Review: Final Report' (2008). Available at: www.border.gov.au/WorkinginAustralia/Documents/457-integrity-review.pdf

Department of Immigration and Citizenship, 'Annual Report' (2000–13)

Department of Immigration and Citizenship, 'Working Holiday and Work and Holiday Visa Report 2005–06 to 2009–10 Program Years' (2005–10)

Department of Immigration and Citizenship, 'Subclass 457 State/Territory Summary Report' (2007–13)

Department of Immigration and Citizenship, 'Australian Migration Trends 2011–12' (2012)

Department of Immigration and Citizenship, 'Student Visa Program Quarterly Report Quarter Ending at 30 June 2013' (2013)

Department of Immigration and Citizenship, 'Working Holiday Maker Visa Program Report Ending at 30 June 2013' (2013)

Faulkner, David, 'The Unequal Treatment of New Zealanders in Australia' (2013). Available at: papers.ssrn.com/sol3/papers.cfm?abstract_id=2304476

Jackling, Beverly, 'The Lure of Permanent Residency and the Aspirations and Expectations of International Students Studying Accounting in Australia' (2007) 15 *People and Place* 31

Khoo, Siew-Ean, Graeme Hugo and Peter McDonald, 'Which Skilled Temporary Migrants Become Permanent Residents and Why?' (2008) 42 *International Migration Review* 193

Knight, Michael, 'Strategic Review of the Student Visa Program 2011' (Report to the Australian Government, June 2011)

Mares, Peter, 'A Routine Removal' (2007) 18 *Griffith Review* 205

Mares, Peter, 'A Special Category' (2014) 43 *Griffith Review*. Available at: griffithreview.com/articles/9677/

Migration Council Australia, 'More Than Temporary: Australia's 457 Visa Program' (2013)

National Centre for Immunisation Research and Surveillance, 'Biennial Report: January 2010–November 2011' (2012). Available at: www.ncirs.edu.au/assets/publications/reports/NCIRS-biennial-report-2010-2011.pdf

Robertson, Shanthi, *Transnational Student-Migrants and the State: The Education–Migration Nexus* (Palgrave Macmillan, 2013)

Ruhs, Martin, *The Price of Rights: Regulating International Labour Migration* (Princeton University Press, 2013)

Tilbrook, Cindy, 'International Students: Perspectives and Graduate Outcomes' (Australian International Education Conference, 2007)

Walzer, Michael, *Spheres of Justice: A Defense of Pluralism and Equality* (Basic Books, 1983)

Legislation

Australian Citizenship Act 2007 (Cth)

Fair Entitlements Guarantee Act 2012 (Cth)

Family And Community Services Legislation Amendment (New Zealand Citizens) Bill 2001

Health Insurance Act 1973 (Cth)

Migration Act 1958 (Cth)

Migration Legislation Amendment Regulation (No 1) 2013 (Cth)

Migration Regulations 1994 (Cth)

National Disability Insurance Scheme Act 2013 (Cth)

Workers Rehabilitation and Compensation Act 2014 (NT)

Other

Australian Bureau of Statistics, *Series 6202: Labour Force, Australia*. Available at: www.abs.gov.au/ausstats/abs%40.nsf/mf/6202.0

Citizenship and Immigration Canada, *Become a Permanent Resident: Live-in Caregivers* (19 October 2012). Available at: www.cic.gc.ca/english/work/caregiver/permanent_resident.asp

Commonwealth of Australia, *Additional Estimates (AE14/217)* Programe 1.1 Visa and Migration (25 February 2014)

Department of Health, Victorian Government, *Free Vaccine Victoria-Criteria For Eligibility*. Available at: www.health.vic.gov.au/immunisation/free-vaccine.htm (site discontinued)

Department of Human Services, Australian Government, *Ex-Gratia Assistance For New Zealand Non-Protected Special Category Visa Holders: New South Wales Floods January 2013*. Available at: www.humanservices.gov.au/spw/customer/forms/resources/em039-130215en.pdf (site discontinued)

Department of Human Services, Australian Government, *Ex-Gratia Assistance for New Zealand Non-Protected Special Category Visa Holders: Queensland Floods January 2013*. Available at: www.humanservices.gov.au/spw/customer/forms/resources/em037-130212en.pdf (site discontinued)

Department of Human Services, Australian Government, *Ex-Gratia Income Support Allowance for New Zealand Non-Protected Special Category Visa Holders: NSW Bushfires October 2013*. Available at:

www.humanservices.gov.au/customer/enablers/centrelink/disaster-recovery-allowance/ex-gratia-income-support-allowance-nsw-bushfires-oct-2013#a4 (site discontinued)

Department of Human Services, Australian Government, *New South Wales Bushfires: October 2013*. Available at: www.humanservices.gov.au/customer/services/centrelink/dra-nsw-bushfires-october-2013

Department of Human Services, Australian Government, *New Zealand Citizens Claiming Payments in Australia*. Available at: www.humanservices.gov.au/customer/enablers/nz-citizens-claiming-payments-in-australia

Department of Human Services, Australian Government, *Newly Arrived Resident's Waiting Period*. Available at: www.humanservices.gov.au/customer/enablers/newly-arrived-residents-waiting-period

Department of Human Services, Australian Government, *Western Australia Bushfires: January 2014*. Available at: www.humanservices.gov.au/customer/enablers/centrelink/australian-government-disaster-recovery-payment/western-australia-bushfires-january-2014 (site discontinued)

Department of Immigration and Border Protection, *Temporary Graduate Visa (subclass 485)*. Available at: www.immi.gov.au/Visas/Pages/485.aspx (site discontinued)

Department of Immigration and Border Protection, *Temporary Work (Skilled) (subclass 457) Visa Information Booklet*. Available at: www.immi.gov.au/allforms/booklets/books9.pdf (site discontinued)

Department of Immigration and Citizenship, *Temporary Entrants and NZ Citizens in Australia*, Quarterly Reports (2011–13)

Department of Immigration and Border Protection, *Ministerial Intervention* (14 May 2014). Available at: www.immi.gov.au/refugee/ministerial_intervention.htm

Donnell, Hayden, 'New Zealand Pair Upset at Flood Cash "Racism"', *New Zealand Herald*, 21 January 2011. Available at: www.nzherald.co.nz/nz/news/article.cfm?c_id=1&objectid=10701102

The Economist, 'Winning the West', 16 March 2013. Available at: www.economist.com/news/asia/21573609-prime-minister-canvasses-fast-changing-suburbs-winning-west

Email from Les Koopowitz to the author (23 October 2013)

Heather, Ben, 'Kiwis' Australian Care Case Settled', *Stuff NZ*, 25 October 2012. Available at: www.stuff.co.nz/world/australia/7858803/Kiwis-Australian-care-case-settled

Heffernan, Madeleine and Clay Lucas, 'International Students Taken to the Cleaners', *The Age*, 2 June 2013. Available at: www.theage.com.au/national/international-students-taken-to-the-cleaners-20130601-2nily.html#ixzz2iQHeVVzW

Howard, John, Speech at the Federal Liberal Party Campaign Launch (28 October 2001)

Interview with Claire Hewitt (29 August 2013)

Mares, Peter, 'Lives On Hold', *Inside Story*, 2 May 2011. Available at: inside.org.au/lives-on-hold/

Mares, Peter, 'Temporary Migration is a Permanent Thing', *Inside Story*, 20 March 2013. Available at: inside.org.au/temporary-migration-is-a-permanent-thing/

Mares, Peter, 'We Know About the 457. What About the 485?' *Inside Story*, 28 March 2013. Available at: inside.org.au/we-know-about-the-457-what-about-the-485/

Mares, Peter, 'Falling Between the Cracks of Temporary Migration', *Inside Story*, 1 November 2013. Available at: inside.org.au/falling-between-the-cracks-of-temporary-migration/

McMillan, Kate and Paul Harmer, 'Kiwis in Australia Deserve Better', *New Zealand Herald*, 10 October 2013. Available at: www.nzherald.co.nz/nz/news/article.cfm?c_id=1&objectid=11137557

Melbourne School of Population and Global Health, Indigenous Eye Health Unit, *The Trachoma Story Kit*. Available at: iehu.unimelb.edu.au/the_trachoma_story_kit/introduction

Morrison, Scott, 'Our Nation' (Address to the 2011 Federation of Ethnic Community Councils of Australia Conference, Adelaide, 18 November 2011). Available at: australianpolitics. com/2011/11/18/morrison-promises-to-protect-the-borders-of-our-values.html#more-4574

Morrison, Scott, 'Doing Far More to Build Our Nation' (Address to the Affinity Intercultural Foundation, Sydney, 17 July 2013). Available at: www.affinity.org.au/wp-content/uploads/2013/07/Morrison-Doing-far-more-to-build-our-nation-170713.pdf

Morrison, Scott, 'Reasons to Be Optimistic about Australia's Immigration Future' (Speech at the Affinity Intercultural Foundation, Sydney, 17 July 2013)

The National Health Performance Authority, *Healthy Communities: Immunization Rates for Children in 2012–13*. Available at: www. myhealthycommunities.gov.au/Content/publications/downloads/ NHPA_HC_Report_Imm_Rates_March_2014.pdf

The National Health Performance Authority, 'Childhood Immunisation Rates Up, But Some Areas Still Low', (Media Release, 24 March 2014)

New Zealand High Commission Canberra, Australia, *Floods Assistance*. Available at: www.nzembassy.com/australia/news/queensland-floods-assistance (site discontinued)

NHMRC Centre for Research Excellence in Population Health, *Protecting Australia: Closing the Gap in Immunisation for Migrants and Refugees: Proceedings from a Stakeholder Workshop*. Available at: www.creimmunisation.com.au/sites/ default/files/newsevents/events/CREMigrantRefugeeWorkshop_ ProceedingsRecommendations.pdf

Radio New Zealand News, *Some Kiwi Students to Get Australian Loans*. Available at: www.radionz.co.nz/news/political/235456/some-kiwi-students-to-get-australian-loans

Tham, Joo-Cheong, 'Multiculturalism and Temporary Migration: Where Does Justice Fit?' (Presentation to Australian Multicultural Commission roundtable, Melbourne, 15 March 2013)

United Voice, *Swan Cleaning Services Update* (5 June 2013). Available at: www.unitedvoice.org.au/news/swan-cleaning-services-update

5

Reconsidering What Constitutes Objective Decision-making About Children Crossing International Borders

Joanne Kinslor[1]

This chapter discusses unintended consequences that arise from the application of Australia's child custody visa requirement referred to as Public Interest Criterion 4015 (PIC 4015). It questions whether the requirement serves the role for which it was designed, both in terms of the nature and the outcomes of decision-making it supports.

PIC 4015 requires that unless all parents/guardians can and do consent to a child's travel to Australia, in most cases a child's ability to travel to Australia will be determined by reference to the law of their home country.

As the policy of the Department of Immigration and Border Protection (DIBP) explains, the primary purpose of this child custody requirement is to ensure that Australia does not facilitate international child abduction. PIC 4015 seeks to give effect to Australia's international obligations, especially those under the Hague Convention on the Civil Aspects of International Child Abduction (the Hague Convention).

---

1   The author is grateful to Emeritus Professor Reg Graycar for her comments.

The High Court case of *Tahiri v Minister for Immigration and Citizenship* (*Tahiri*) highlights how a provision designed to protect the welfare of children through preventing child abduction can have the effect of preventing children coming to Australia where no issue of child abduction arises and where the Hague Convention does not apply.

While PIC 4015 was said to introduce an objective test for determining child custody, *Tahiri* demonstrates how the provision's focus upon the family law of foreign countries instead facilitates discrimination against women.

Introduction

The case of *Tahiri* raises the question of how a law (PIC 4015) designed for the protection of children led to a family of refugees (comprising a sole parent — an Afghan Hazara woman — and her children) being refused humanitarian visas. How could the only reason for refusal of their visas and migration to the safety of Australia be that they failed to meet a visa requirement designed to uphold international law for the protection of children?

Learning that this result arose because Australian law gave effect to Afghan family law raises the further query of why Australia, a country committed to sex equality,[2] would maintain a law giving effect to a strongly patriarchal system of law. This law, characterised as an objective test for deciding child custody issues between parents/ guardians, instead prioritised the custody rights of a missing and absent father while denying the rights and responsibility of a mother engaged in full-time care for those children.

This chapter considers whether such results constitute the unintended, but necessary, consequences of Australia upholding the Hague Convention. It concludes that the law is inconsistent with the terms of the Hague Convention and is not justified on the basis that Australia needs to uphold its obligations under the convention. Rather, for the reasons outlined below, it suggests that Australia should be concerned

---

2   Notably, in the migration context, all applicants for Australian visas are required to acknowledge an Australian values statement, which includes the following: 'Australian society values respect for … equality of men and women'. *Migration Regulations 1994* (Cth) sch 4 item 4019.

that the law impedes our nation in upholding international law, such as our obligations under the Convention on the Rights of the Child, which requires that the best interests of children be a primary consideration in administrative decision-making, and the Convention on the Elimination of All Forms of Discrimination against Women.

The chapter begins by discussing the facts of the High Court case of *Tahiri* and the terms of the law that applied in that case, PIC 4015. The discussion focuses upon the unintended and interrelated impacts of applying PIC 4015, which excludes consideration of the best interests of children to whom it applies and discriminates against women. The chapter explains how PIC 4015 was designed with Australia's obligations under the Hague Convention as a main concern, but that the limited considerations permitted by its terms do not allow assessment of when the Hague Convention applies or the exceptional circumstances covered by the convention. The chapter concludes that decision-makers require further scope to consider relevant factors if they are to be equipped to make decisions upholding policy objectives and Australian international legal obligations amongst the varied and complex cases that inevitably arise about children crossing international borders.

The Case: *Tahiri v Minister for Immigration and Citizenship* [2012] HCA 61
13 December 2012, 293 ALR 526

Tahiri concerned an offshore humanitarian visa application by an Afghan Hazara woman, Mrs Tahiri.[3] In early 2003, Mrs Tahiri's husband left the family in Jaghori, Ghazni province, Afghanistan, to travel to the province of Kandahar. Mrs Tahiri was pregnant with their sixth child at the time her husband left, and this child was born later in the same year.

---

3   The summary of facts is taken from the written submissions the plaintiff and the defendant submitted to the High Court in *Tahiri v Minister for Immigration and Citizenship Case No. M77/2012*. Available at: www.hcourt.gov.au/cases/cases_m77-2012. Facts are also from the judgement of the High Court *Tahiri v Minister for Immigration and Citizenship* (2012) 293 ALR 526.

Mrs Tahiri had no contact from her husband after his departure and no communication from any source about his whereabouts or welfare. After losing contact with her husband she travelled to Pakistan with all her children in 2003. They lived together as refugees in Quetta, Pakistan, without any right of residence, until at least 2012. Quetta is a city where many thousands of Afghan Hazaras have fled to escape persecution, particularly on account of atrocities committed by the Taliban against Hazaras.[4]

In 2009, Mrs Tahiri's eldest son, Javed Hussain (the plaintiff in the High Court case), travelled to Australia as an unaccompanied minor. He was recognised as a refugee and granted a protection visa permitting him to live in Australia permanently. He proposed his mother for an offshore humanitarian visa,[5] which included his siblings. Mrs Tahiri's visa application was refused on 2 January 2012 because she could not satisfy the delegate considering the application that she had custody of her four youngest children[6] in the terms required by the migration regulations. Specifically, Mrs Tahiri was refused her visa because her children under 18 years of age did not meet PIC 4015, which is discussed in detail below.[7] This requirement is distinct from the requirements specific to the visa being applied for — in Mrs Tahiri's case, a humanitarian visa that required that she was the parent of a person who held a protection visa (her son, Javed).

Mrs Tahiri's uncontradicted evidence was that she had moved her children from Afghanistan to Pakistan and had cared for them as a sole parent for almost nine years, since her husband went missing. The delegate accepted that her husband had been missing since 2003 and had no involvement with the children since then. Before the High Court it was pointed out that, given Quetta is a place where many Afghan Hazaras have fled to escape the Taliban, it would have been an obvious location for her husband to search for his family if he were

---

4   See, for example, UK Home Office, 'Pakistan Country of Origin Information (COI) Report' (9 August 2013) 172–174.

5   Subclass 202 Refugee and Humanitarian (Class XB) visa.

6   Her eldest daughter was married and not included in the visa application when it was decided.

7   Specifically *Migration Regulations 1994* (Cth) sch 2 cl 202.228. This criterion required Mrs Tahiri to establish that each member of her family unit who had not turned 18 and had made a combined visa application with her satisfied PIC 4015 (and 4016) before she was eligible for her visa. In addition, each of the children had to meet equivalent criteria (PIC 4017 and 4018) to be eligible for their visas.

alive. Since he had been missing for more than seven years, it was argued that the common law presumption of death applied — that is, a person will be presumed dead if they have been missing for a period of at least seven years.[8]

The delegate refused the visa without deciding whether Mrs Tahiri's husband was alive or dead. He first found that the applicable law governing custody of the children was the law of Afghanistan (not Pakistan). He found that if her husband were alive, under Afghan law he had the right to determine where the children were to live and if he were dead that right passed to his family. The delegate (who was not required to provide reasons for his decision)[9] is recorded as concluding:

> In both Afghan law and custom, the custody of the minor children would fall to the father's side if there were credible and substantial evidence of the death of the father ...[10]

Nothing more specific than that conclusion was given. No source references were provided for the delegate's understanding of Afghan law and custom. His conclusion as to how Afghan law and custom operated was not challenged[11] by the plaintiff nor referenced by the defendant. In oral submissions, the solicitor general noted that the delegate was based in Dubai and 'probably had many applications of this kind' and 'had built up a knowledge base or view of Afghan law'.[12]

Nor was the finding any more specific than custody going to the 'father's side' if Mrs Tahiri's husband were dead. No specific member of the family or type of relationship was identified. Given the

---

8   Javed Hussain Tahiri, 'Plaintiff's Submission', Submission in *Tahiri v Minister for Immigration and Citizenship*, No M77/2012, 21 November 2012, 15. The plaintiff references the common law presumption of death as *Axon v Axon* (1937) 59 CLR 395, 404–405 (Dixon J).

9   The delegate was only required to notify Mrs Tahiri of the criterion that was not satisfied and led to refusal of the visa. *Migration Act 1958* (Cth) s66. The findings of the delegate discussed were drawn from records in the file. See *Tahiri v Minister for Immigration and Citizenship* (2012) 293 ALR 526, 9.

10   Javed Hussain Tahiri, 'Plaintiff's Submission', Submission in *Tahiri v Minister for Immigration and Citizenship*, No M77/2012, 21 November 2012, 9.

11   It must be noted that the review before the High Court of Australia was limited to judicial review on the grounds of jurisdictional error — not merits review. A decision-maker can commit a jurisdictional error by making a finding of fact for which there is no evidence. The plaintiff in *Tahiri* did not argue that the decision-maker had no evidence for this finding.

12   *Tahiri v Minister for Immigration and Citizenship* [2012] HCATrans 336 (7 December 2012) 44.

patriarchal flavour of the law identified by the delegate as applying, it was implicitly assumed that the 'father's side' meant male members of the father's family, and it was noted in oral submissions before the High Court that the father had brothers who were alive,[13] but nothing was established in terms of contact between Mrs Tahiri's children and their paternal uncles, any involvement by the uncles in the children's lives, or any interest by the uncles in the children's whereabouts or welfare.[14]

The High Court decided unanimously[15] that the finding was sufficient for the visa to be refused on account of a failure to meet child custody requirements.[16] The fact that 'the mother had had sole parental responsibility for the four children for nearly nine years ... because the father had gone missing in Afghanistan in 2003', was not disputed.[17] However, it was not sufficient to establish that the delegate's conclusion was erroneous. The High Court upheld the delegate's decision as valid.

It is important to note that the High Court was not ruling upon the merits or the justice of the delegate's decision, but only upon whether the delegate had made a serious legal error (a jurisdictional error) in making his decision. Nor did the High Court rule that the delegate's conclusions were the only conclusions that could be lawfully made. The High Court found that it was open for the delegate to form the conclusions he did,[18] while not precluding that alternative lawful findings could have been made.[19] This paper does not seek to analyse the legal arguments and administrative law principles relevant to the decision. It considers *Tahiri* for the purpose of examining how

---

13   Ibid., 44, 45.

14   In oral submissions it was noted that evidence had been given that the uncles did not give them any assistance in Afghanistan. Ibid., 44.

15   The matter was heard by French CJ, Bell and Gaegler JJ who wrote a joint judgement.

16   There were two relevant requirements: PIC 4015 and PIC 4016. Both had to be met for the visa to be granted, so failure to meet PIC 4015 meant PIC 4016 did not need to be considered. These requirements are discussed below.

17   *Tahiri v Minister for Immigration and Citizenship* [2012] HCATrans 336 (7 December 2012) 12, 13. This was a summary of evidence accepted by the delegate and not challenged by the defendant.

18   To make his case, the plaintiff had to establish that it was not open for the delegate to come to the conclusions he did on the material that was before the delegate. This was necessary to show that the delegate had committed an error of law in circumstances in which there was no requirement for the delegate to provide reasons for his decision.

19   That would be a matter of hypothetical speculation irrelevant to the consideration of whether the decision made was valid. The significance is that other decision-makers considering similar situations may be able to make lawful decisions with differing conclusions.

PIC 4015 operates and argues that the criterion operates in a manner that is blind to its effects in compounding discrimination against women and excluding consideration of the best interests of children.[20]

Public Interest Criterion 4015

Tahiri was solely focused upon the operation of PIC 4015.[21] This criterion requires that, for a visa applicant under the age of 18, at least one of the following applies:

1. the law of the visa applicant's home country permits her/his removal;
2. each person who can lawfully determine where the applicant is to live consents to the grant of the visa; or
3. the grant of the visa would be consistent with an Australian child order.[22]

PIC 4015 is accompanied by PIC 4016, which requires that, for visa applicants under 18, there is no compelling reason why grant of the visa would not be in the best interests of that child.[23] The requirements are common to almost all Australian visas.[24] They are not confined to humanitarian/refugee visas.

PIC 4015 is a requirement for the primary visa applicant, who will be the family head for the purpose of the visa application. If a child under 18 does not have permission to travel in the terms required by PIC 4015, it is not only the child who will be refused a visa for travel,

---

20   As noted below, the best interests of children is central to an additional visa requirement, PIC 4016. However, since 4015 and 4016 are separate and additional to each other, the best interests of children may be completely excluded from a decision made by reference to the interests of children, as in *Tahiri*. Therefore, when a matter is refused for failure to meet PIC 4015, there is no consideration of the best interests of the children as per PIC 4016.

21   *Migration Regulations 1994* (Cth) sch 4, item 4015.

22   An Australian child order in PIC 4015(c) is defined as an order under s70L(1) of the *Family Law Act 1975* (Cth), which covers parenting orders made by Australian courts in relation to who a child is to live with and spend time with. (See *Tahiri v Minister for Immigration and Citizenship* (2012) 293 ALR 526, 6.) It was not relevant in *Tahiri* and is unlikely to be relevant for visa applicants outside Australia, but it is an important additional option for visa applicants able to access Australian courts.

23   PIC 4015 and 4016 apply to a primary visa applicant. PIC 4017 and 4018 are in the same terms, but apply to secondary visa applicants.

24   The onshore subclass 866 protection visa is an exception. Applicants for a subclass 866 visa are not required to meet PIC 4015, 4016, 4017, or 4018.

but also the primary applicant, who is usually a parent of the child. Therefore, in Mrs Tahiri's case, she and her children were refused humanitarian visas to come to Australia because the children did not have appropriate permission to travel.

The law of the home country

'Home country' in PIC 4015(a) is defined in the regulations[25] as being a person's country of citizenship, unless the person is usually resident in another country and not usually resident in her or his country of citizenship. The default position is that the country of citizenship is the home country and can only cease to be so if the person is not usually resident there (although that is not sufficient): '[A] person may not be "usually resident" in the person's country of citizenship without necessarily being "usually a resident" of another country.'[26] The person's home country will only become different to their country of citizenship if she or he is usually a resident of another country.

The High Court directed that 'usually resident' in PIC 4015 should be approached as a broad factual inquiry, such as that of 'habitual residence' in the Hague Convention, taking into account 'the actual and intended length of stay in a state, the purpose of the stay, the strength of ties to the state and to any other state (both in the past and currently), [and] the degree of assimilation into the state'.[27]

In *Tahiri*, the delegate found that the children's home country was their country of citizenship, Afghanistan, and the High Court upheld that approach. Although the children had lived in Pakistan since 2003 (over six years before the visa application was made), the High Court identified countervailing factors (the circumstances of their arrival in Pakistan as refugees, their being illegal residents of Pakistan, and their having visited Afghanistan) as sufficient to leave it open for the delegate to find, as a matter of fact, that Afghanistan was the children's home country, and that they were not usually residents of Pakistan.[28]

---

25   *Migration Regulations 1994* (Cth) reg 1.03.
26   *Tahiri v Minister for Immigration and Citizenship* (2012) 293 ALR 526, 15.
27   Ibid., 16.
28   Ibid., 17.

As noted above, it was then sufficient for the delegate to use his general knowledge of Afghan law to decide that it did not permit the removal of Mrs Tahiri's children. Nothing was established as to any specific inquiries made by the delegate of relevant experts and the file did not record any specific reference material referred to by the delegate.[29]

Mrs Tahiri was given an opportunity to provide court orders from Afghanistan, but was unable to produce any — only submitting a document entitled 'Aram High Court, Kabul, Afghanistan', which she later admitted she had obtained by paying money to a person she did not know and which was not accepted as a genuine court document.[30]

Personal consent of relevant persons

For PIC 4015(b) to be satisfied, a delegate must first determine which persons have custody/residence rights in relation to a child and then ensure that consent is provided by each of those persons. Department policy requires written consent. This limb can never be satisfied if a relevant person is unable or unwilling to provide consent, and it is up to the parent wanting to bring the child to Australia to prove this consent.

Department policy directs that where there is no evidence of any other person having custody/residence responsibility, then delegates 'should presume that the [sponsoring] parent is the only person who needs to consent to the visa grant'. However, this is balanced by the directive that a 'non-custodial parent' who has not had contact with the child for a long time (or cannot be located) may not be assumed to consent and may have rights in relation to the child. Therefore, before a delegate can conclude that there is no evidence of someone not involved in the visa application having rights the law of the relevant country should be considered.

---

29   As a matter of law, it was up to Mrs Tahiri to establish that the law of the home country permitted travel and a lack of evidence would create a default position where the delegate would not be satisfied. See the Full Federal Court's discussion in *Minister for Immigration & Multicultural & Indigenous Affairs v VSAF of 2003* [2005] FCAFC 73 (10 May 2005) in relation to a requirement to be satisfied.
30   Refer to *Tahiri v Minister for Immigration and Citizenship* (2012) 293 ALR 526, 10.

In *Tahiri*, the plaintiff argued that PIC 4015(b) should be determined according to Australian law and Australian notions of parental responsibility and guardianship, not the law of Afghanistan.[31] Applying Australian law meant that the parents had the right to determine whether the children could come to Australia, but since the father could have no parental responsibility for the children (having been missing for many years), and since he should be presumed dead (having been missing for more than seven years), the only person who needed to provide consent was Mrs Tahiri.

The High Court did not accept that submission and held that the legal ability of a person to determine where a child applicant is to live 'may arise under any system of law that governs the relationship between such a person and the additional applicant'.[32] The court held that it was open to the delegate to decide that consent was needed either from the father or his relatives as this was required by Afghan law.[33]

'A more objective test'? Identifying the biases embedded in the terms of PIC 4015

PIC 4015 and 4016 were introduced by legislative amendments commencing 1 July 2000[34] and replaced a requirement that the grant of a visa 'would not prejudice the rights and interests of any other person who has custody or guardianship of, or access to' a dependent child included in a visa application.[35] The only explanation for the change (included in the explanatory statement) was that the new criteria provided 'a more objective test for decision-makers'.[36]

---

31   *Tahiri v Minister for Immigration and Citizenship* [2012] HCATrans 336 (7 December 2012) 7, 8.

32   *Tahiri v Minister for Immigration and Citizenship* (2012) 293 ALR 526, 18.

33   Ibid., 21.

34   *Migration Amendment Regulations 2000 (No. 2)* (Cth) sch 3 pt 3.5 item 3506.

35   This requirement was included in Schedule 2 criteria for individual visas, rather than being located in Schedule 4 of the regulations. See, for example, former sub-regulation 202.228, requiring: 'If the family unit of the applicant includes a dependent child whose application was combined with the applicant's, the Minister is satisfied that the grant of the visa to the child would not prejudice the rights and interests of any other person who has custody or guardianship of, or access to, the child.'

36   Explanatory Memorandum, *Migration Amendment Regulations 2000 (No. 2)* (Cth). No explanation as to what purportedly made it a more objective test was provided.

It is not apparent how the amended form of PIC 4015 is a more objective test. Both tests require a decision-maker to make factual determinations uninfluenced by their feelings or personal opinions. In the former test, whether prejudice or detriment would be caused to the rights and interests of a person is a question of fact specific to the circumstances of an individual case. The decision-maker needed to determine whether prejudice arises in a particular case. In the absence of an explanation, it may be that the concern was that the word 'prejudice' required potentially complex assessment of the context of a case and called for a judgement to be made by the decision-maker as to the nature of any prejudice arising in a case. Reflecting this, previous policy for decision-makers applying the previous law stated 'it is unlikely that granting a permanent visa to a child would be seen as prejudicing a person's access rights of, say, two weeks a year'.

A concern with the unexplained assertion that the test is more objective is that, used as a justification in support of the change, it implies that the current test is more neutral in how it applies to different visa applicants. *Tahiri* highlights how this is not the case. The test indirectly discriminates against women by giving effect to foreign laws that directly discriminate against women.[37] Australia is a signatory to the Convention on the Elimination of All Forms of Discrimination against Women (CEDAW). The Australian Human Rights Commission explains: 'In signing CEDAW, Australia committed itself to being a society that promotes policies, laws, organisation, structures and attitudes that ensure women are guaranteed the same rights as men.'[38] Yet, our immigration law is operating to give effect to the directly discriminatory law of a country notorious for inequitable treatment of women and to the discriminatory laws of other countries.[39]

---

37 Regina Graycar and Jenny Morgan, *The Hidden Gender of Law* (Federation Press, 2nd edition, 2002) 28, 29.

38 Australian Human Rights Commission, *The Convention on the Elimination of All Forms of Discrimination against Women (CEDAW): Sex Discrimination – International Activities.* Available at: www.humanrights.gov.au/convention-elimination-all-forms-discrimination-against-women-cedaw-sex-discrimination-international.

39 While I have not researched the number of countries with such laws, secondary material records that it is not only the women of Afghanistan who are directly discriminated against by their country's family law. See, for example, Akanksha Sharma and Harini Viswanathan, 'Extension of the Hague Convention to Non-Signatory Nations: A Possible Solution to Parental Child Abduction' (2011) 4 *International Journal of Private Law* 546.

Regina Graycar and Jenny Morgan discuss different approaches to understanding the meaning of gender equality, including formal equality, in which everyone is treated the same regardless of their gender, and special treatment, where women are treated differently because of their difference.[40] PIC 4015 is an example of the limits of formal equality. The terms of PIC 4015 do not treat women and men differently, but, as illustrated by *Tahiri,* PIC 4015 relies upon foreign state law that may place women and men in very different positions, and it is on account of this socially constructed difference that women and men are treated unequally. Yet, a special treatment approach creates unnecessary complexity in this case because the inequality operating is that of a foreign law. To afford women special treatment because of that foreign law is to continue to afford the law an operation within Australian law that is not required. Graycar and Morgan track the influence of Catherine MacKinnon's subordination approach to inequality, which analyses gender difference as a matter of differentiation in power between men and women. Under this model, we are able to consider the operation of PIC 4015 as compounding the powerlessness of women in context — a context that includes the position of women in Afghan law and society. This focuses attention upon the fault in PIC 4015 of giving operation to foreign law from a context with societal norms of deeply entrenched sex inequality contrary to Australian values and commitments.

While Australian immigration law impacts upon individuals outside Australia, its jurisdiction is Australia (a permission to enter and remain in Australia) and, as outlined below, Australia's international legal obligations do not require that Australia give unqualified effect to foreign legal systems.

Furthermore, indirect discrimination arises where the law of a child's home country is unable or unwilling to protect women from family violence. Women in such situations need protection for themselves and their children. PIC 4015 requires them either to obtain permission from their abusive husband/partner, or to obtain permission from the state that is failing to protect them — which may include a failure by the state to even acknowledge their right to be protected from their

---

40   Ibid., 37.

husband/partner.[41] No consideration of circumstances is permitted. PIC 4015 gives further effect to such patriarchal systems of law and government within Australian law. It fails to recognise that women in such situations are not equal before the law and by consequence will not have an equal opportunity to obtain the right to determine where their children should live.

MacKinnon writes that 'objectivity — the non-situated, universal standpoint, whether claimed or aspired to — is a denial of the existence or potency of sex inequality that tacitly participates in constructing reality from the dominant point of view'.[42] PIC 4015 gives effect — 'objectively' — to foreign state law without any evaluation of the effect of the law. Justifying this approach as good law because it is 'more objective' denies the sex inequality of foreign state laws and, by consequence, the sex inequality of PIC 4015.

PIC 4015(a) is concerned only with the operation of foreign state law. PIC 4015(b) is concerned only with 'persons who can lawfully determine where' a child is to live. The High Court has explained this requirement as referring to a 'legal ability' to determine where a child may live that may arise 'under any system of law that governs the relationship between' the person and the child.[43] Thus, PIC 4015 may determine the question of child custody (a family matter) by reference to the public law of a foreign state while simultaneously failing to give any weight to the reality of what is occurring in the private sphere of the relevant family (unless that is recognised by the applicable state law).[44] While *Tahiri* does not provide a thorough

---

41   The serious harm that a woman may face in such circumstances and her need for protection by the international community has been recognised in Australia through acknowledgement that the Refugee Convention can apply to such situations. See, in particular, *Minister for Immigration v Khawar* (2002) 210 CLR 1.

42   Catherine MacKinnon, 'Feminism, Marxism, Method, and the State: Toward Feminist Jurisprudence' (1983) 8 *Signs: Journal of Women in Culture and Society* 635.

43   *Tahiri v Minister for Immigration and Citizenship* (2012) 293 ALR 526, 18.

44   There is a considerable body of feminist legal theory showing that the public/private distinction has been used in law to justify non-intervention by the state for the protection and advancement of women, while also creating gendered hierarchies within the private sphere: '[T]he crucial impact of feminist scholarship on family research has been to recast the family as a system of gender stratification. Because roles neglect the political underpinning of the family, feminists have directed attention outside the family "to the social structures that shape experience and meaning, that give people a location in the social world, and that define and allocate economic and social rewards".' Zinn quoting Hess and Marz Ferree in Maxine Baca, 'Family, Feminism and Race in America' in Nancy E Dowd and Michelle S Jacobs (eds), *Feminist Legal Theory* (New York University Press, 2003).

examination of Afghan law, it presents a situation in which a woman may have sole custody/parental responsibility of her children within the private sphere of the family but no legal ability arising under an applicable system of law to determine where those children may live.[45] This law subjugates the interests of a woman to her absent husband (and his family), and the logic of PIC 4015 is that using this law is an objective and rational manner of determining child custody because it is public law.[46]

The consequences arising from the application of PIC 4015 in such a situation can be further illustrated by considering the hypothetical scenario of the death of Mrs Tahiri's husband being established and her husband's family deciding to take the children to Australia without her. In such a situation, PIC 4015 would give effect to the custody rights of the husband's family while it may fail to recognise the need for Mrs Tahiri's consent because her custody rights/parental responsibilities do not arise under a system of public state law. Such an effect demonstrates how PIC 4015's focus upon custody rights as determined by public state law not only disempowers women based in the private sphere, but also operates without reference to them.[47]

Tahiri further illustrates how a law designed for the benefit of children does not include any consideration of the child's interests or perspectives. The terms of PIC 4015 are about matters affecting the child but not the child herself or himself. The law situates the

---

45   Javed Hussain Tahiri, 'Plaintiff's Submission', Submission in *Tahiri v Minister for Immigration and Citizenship*, No M77/2012, 21 November 2012, 9. Having viewed the file, the plaintiff states that the decision-maker in *Tahiri* implicitly found that the mother was not a person who solely or jointly could lawfully determine where the children were to live. While the focus of the case was not on whether the mother had any such legal right (because it was clear she consented to the children's travel) the only legal ability to determine where the children could live identified in the case was that of the father and the father's family.

46   This reflects a notion, critiqued by feminists, of the public sphere as rational, in contrast to the private sphere as irrational and particular. See, for example, Margaret Thornton, 'The Cartography of Public and Private' in Margaret Thornton (ed.), *Public and Private Feminist Legal Debates* (Oxford University Press, 1994).

47   In such a scenario, PIC 4016 would then need to be considered. It requires consideration as to whether there is a compelling reason to believe that grant of a visa would not be in the best interests of a child. Mrs Tahiri's ability to travel with the children would be relevant to such a consideration. However, that is not a sufficient remedy for the shortcomings of PIC 4015 in failing to acknowledge and consider Mrs Tahiri's role and importance to the children, which in this hypothetical scenario creates a terrible situation of considering the best interests of children in escaping persecution as against their interests in being with their mother who has been their sole carer for many years.

child only as subject to law and the will of others, not as a subject in her/his own right. Given this approach, it is unsurprising that it supports outcomes such as in *Tahiri* where children in an incredibly vulnerable situation were denied humanitarian visas without any consideration of their interests. The case of *Tahiri* is only one example of the operation of this law, which applies to skilled visa applicants, family visa applicants and business visa applicants.[48]

A re-evaluation of PIC 4015 is required by reference to the objectives sought to be achieved by the requirement.

Reconsidering the objectives of PIC 4015

The policy manual of DIBP discusses the purpose of PIC 4015 as being 'to assist Australia in meeting its obligations as a party to several international conventions relating to the protection of children under 18 years of age, such as the Hague Convention,[49] the Convention on the Rights of the Child (CROC) and the Hague Convention on Protection and Cooperation in Respect of Intercountry Adoption'. The manual's discussion of the background to PIC 4015 further states that '[m]igration law requires officers to consider the effect that granting a visa to a minor may have on the objectives of the Hague Convention', and identifies the convention's objectives incorporated into Australian domestic law as being to:

i.   secure the prompt return of children wrongfully removed to, or retained in, any 'contracting state' (that is, any country that is a signatory to the Hague Convention), and

ii. ensure that the rights of 'custody' and 'access' under the law of the contracting state are effectively respected in other contracting states.

---

48   There are many interconnections between the interests of women and children. Given the situation raised in *Tahiri*, it is of interest to note an account by Graycar and Morgan of child custody law in Australia. They note a change from absolute custody rights being held by fathers to a situation in which custody was granted to mothers as occurring '[o]nce the equity courts were given power to consider applications for custody from mothers according to principles under which the welfare of the child came to be considered as paramount'. See Regina Graycar and Jenny Morgan, above fn 37, 258.

49   *Convention on the Civil Aspects of International Child Abduction*, 25 October 1980, Hague XXVIII (entered into force 1 December 1983).

The Hague Convention addresses international child abduction by creating a framework for deciding the forum where child custody disputes will be decided. The general operating principle is that a child should be returned to their country of habitual residence for the resolution of a custody dispute. Consistent with this, PIC 4015 gives priority to the law of a person's home country, which was a focus for consideration in *Tahiri*. The problem is that, as the decision in *Tahiri* shows, PIC 4015 has a much broader application than the Hague Convention: it determines custody by reference to a child's home country regardless of whether there is a case of child abduction and regardless of whether the Hague Convention applies.

There was nothing to suggest a child custody dispute arose in the case of *Tahiri* — much to the contrary[50] — yet PIC 4015 stopped Mrs Tahiri bringing her children to Australia. This law has been justified on the basis that it seeks to prevent child abduction yet it does not allow for consideration as to whether there is any prospect of child abduction occurring in cases to which it applies.

Furthermore, PIC 4015 operated to give effect to the law of Afghanistan, notwithstanding that Afghanistan is not a signatory to the Hague Convention. Thus no Hague Convention obligation arose for Australia in the circumstances of the case. Considering the discriminatory effect of PIC 4015, discussed above, and the justification of PIC 4015 as the means by which Australia upholds its Hague Convention obligations, it is of great concern that PIC 4015 prioritises the law of a foreign country regardless of whether that country even claims to adhere to the objectives of the Hague Convention. That convention only applies to children habitually resident in a signatory state.[51] By failing to distinguish between signatory and non-signatory countries, this Australian law gives equal effect to the domestic law of countries

---

50   The facts accepted were that Mrs Tahiri was the only person to have any interest in the children — either in terms of asserting parental rights of custody or taking parental responsibility towards the children (as reflected in modern Australian family law norms concerned not to treat children as property).

51   Javed Hussain Taheri, 'Plaintiff's Submission', Submission in *Tahiri v Minister for Immigration and Citizenship*, No M77/2012, 21 November 2012, 15, 16, referring to the *Convention on the Civil Aspects of International Child Abduction*, 25 October 1980, Hague XXVIII (entered into force 1 December 1983) art 4.

that support the convention and countries that do not, including those countries opposed to the religious and gender neutrality of the convention.[52]

Even where it does apply, the Hague Convention allows for more nuanced consideration of the circumstances of a case to advance its multiplicity of objectives.[53] Balancing the general approach of the convention (that states should facilitate the prompt return of children to their country of habitual residence) are provisions that allow for consideration of exceptional circumstances. Article 13(a) states that there is no obligation to return a child where the petitioner was not caring for the child or exercising custody rights at the time of removal. Article 13(b) states that there is no obligation to return a child where there is a grave risk that the child would be exposed to 'physical or psychological harm' or placed in 'an intolerable situation'. Perhaps most relevantly to *Tahiri*, Article 20 provides that a country may refuse to return a child if return would conflict with the fundamental principles of the state relating to protection of human rights and fundamental freedoms. By contrast, PIC 4015 does not permit consideration of any of these significant matters, and in failing to do so has a practical operation that is contrary to the terms and spirit of the convention in some cases.

---

52   Sharma and Viswanathan state that most Islamic nations have not signed the Hague Convention because of differences such as wanting Sharia law to be a part of decision-making in relation to children. They also explain that for Muslim countries, such as Egypt, fathers are given custody of children after the age of dependence as a matter of law. Akanksha Sharma and Harini Viswanathan, above fn 39. Bowie identifies how Australian Courts have treated cases of child abduction differently, depending upon whether the child has been abducted from a country that is a signatory to the Hague Convention. The difference being that for non-signatory countries the welfare or best interests of the particular child is a paramount consideration, whereas for signatory countries this principle does not apply. She cites the High Court decisions of *ZP v PS* (1994) 122 ALR 1 and *De L v Director General, NSW Department of Community Services* (1996) 187 CLR 640: Krista Bowie, 'International Application and Interpretation of the *Convention on the Civil Aspects of International Child Abduction*' (March 2001).

53   Preamble, *Convention on the Civil Aspects of International Child Abduction*, 25 October 1980, Hague XXVIII (entered into force 1 December 1983). The convention's objectives are to confirm the paramount importance of the interests of children; protect children from wrongful removal or retention; establish procedures for children's prompt return to their state of habitual residence; and seek rights of access.

Conclusion

The High Court's judgement in *Tahiri* focused attention upon the situation of a vulnerable woman and her children unlikely to otherwise come to public attention, while at the same time declaring that Australian law operated to exclude consideration of their personal circumstances from a determination critical to whether they would be permitted to resettle in Australia. Applying PIC 4015 limited consideration of child custody to the question of whether Mrs Tahiri's husband or his family had given consent to the children's travel. In its judgement, the High Court did not engage with the fact that the Afghan law is discriminatory, nor did it acknowledge the substantive responsibility that Mrs Tahiri had exercised as a sole parent in relation to her children. The constraints imposed by the limited nature of review available did not permit consideration of the welfare of the family or the best interests of the children.

It is important that Australia does not facilitate child abduction and seeks to specifically consider the welfare of vulnerable minors in making visa decisions. Achieving these aims in the context of a visa decision can be difficult, especially since it can require consideration of the interests of a party not involved in a visa application.

However, the potential difficulty of achieving such goals does not justify a law preventing consideration of circumstances relevant to a just outcome. The unintended consequences of the operation of PIC 4015 illustrated by *Tahiri* are the likely, perhaps inevitable, consequences of a law that seems to be crafted to minimise or eliminate evaluative and situational judgements in decision-making. The assessment required is about whether facts are in existence (such as whether the law of a home country allows a child to travel or whether parents have provided consent), not whether a child should, in the circumstances of a particular case, be refused a visa because that is likely to facilitate child abduction or be contrary to the interests of children and their parents/guardians. Justifying such an approach as superior because it is more objective denies the biases within the law. Limiting the matters decision-makers are permitted to consider also limits their capacity to make fair decisions.

The unintended consequences of applying PIC 4015 highlighted by, but not limited to, the facts of *Tahiri* should motivate reconsideration of the terms of PIC 4015 to determine how its discriminatory impact upon women and adverse consequences for children may be reduced, and how policy objectives may be better achieved. This may well require acknowledgement of the importance of evaluative judgements and consideration of subjective circumstances, rather than a desire to exclude them from 'objective' decision-making.

Bibliography

Articles, books, and reports

Baca, Maxine, 'Family, Feminism and Race in America' in Nancy E Dowd and Michelle S Jacobs (eds), *Feminist Legal Theory* (New York University Press, 2003)

Graycar, Regina and Jenny Morgan, *The Hidden Gender of Law* (Federation Press, 2nd edition, 2002)

MacKinnon, Catherine, 'Feminism, Marxism, Method, and the State: Toward Feminist Jurisprudence' (1983) 8 *Signs: Journal of Women in Culture and Society* 635

Sharma, Akanksha and Harini Viswanathan, 'Extension of the Hague Convention to Non-Signatory Nations: A Possible Solution to Parental Child Abduction' (2011) 4 *International Journal of Private Law* 546

Thornton, Margaret, 'The Cartography of Public and Private' in Margaret Thornton (ed.), *Public and Private Feminist Legal Debates* (Oxford University Press, 1994)

UK Home Office, 'Pakistan Country of Origin Information (COI) Report' (9 August 2013)

Cases

Axon v Axon (1937) 59 CLR 395

De L v Director General, NSW Department of Community Services (1996) 187 CLR 640

Minister for Immigration & Multicultural & Indigenous Affairs v VSAF of 2003 [2005] FCAFC 73 (10 May 2005)

Minister for Immigration v Khawar (2002) 210 CLR 1 Tahiri, Javed Hussain, 'Plaintiff's Submission', Submission in Tahiri v Minister for Immigration and Citizenship, No M77/2012, 21 November 2012

Tahiri v Minister for Immigration and Citizenship (2012) 293 ALR 526

Tahiri v Minister for Immigration and Citizenship [2012] HCATrans 336 (7 December 2012)

ZP v PS (1994) 122 ALR 1

Legislation

Family Law Act 1975 (Cth)

Migration Act 1958 (Cth)

Migration Amendment Regulations 2000 (No. 2) (Cth)

Migration Regulations 1994 (Cth)

Treaties

Convention on the Civil Aspects of International Child Abduction, 25 October 1980, Hague XXVIII (entered into force 1 December 1983)

Other

Australian Human Rights Commission, *The Convention on the Elimination of All Forms of Discrimination against Women (CEDAW): Sex Discrimination – International Activities.* Available at: www.humanrights.gov.au/convention-elimination-all-forms-discrimination-against-women-cedaw-sex-discrimination-international

Bowie, Krista M, 'International Application and Interpretation of the *Convention on the Civil Aspects of International Child Abduction*' (March 2001). Available at: www.familycourt.gov.au/wps/wcm/connect/872fc343-d6e8-4ab3-84ba-b3f58662ec4e/bowie.pdf?MOD=AJPERES&CONVERT_TO=url&CACHEID=872fc343-d6e8-4ab3-84ba-b3f58662ec4e

Tahiri v Minister for Immigration and Citizenship Case No. M77/2012. Available at: www.hcourt.gov.au/cases/cases_m77-2012

6

A Brief Case for Open Borders in Australia

Benjamin Powell[1]

Australia is a nation of immigrants. Just over 25 per cent of the Australian population is foreign born,[2] and an additional quarter of the population has at least one foreign-born parent. Despite receiving large numbers of migrants, Australia remains sparsely populated. A land rich in natural beauty and resources remains lacking in its quantity of what economist Julian Simon referred to as the ultimate resource: people.[3] Yet, as other papers have discussed, the Australian Government still imposes significant barriers to allowing more immigrants. These barriers limit low-skilled immigration as well as the migration of college-educated and other more skilled workers.

---

1   This chapter draws heavily on some of my prior published writing and modifies it to reflect my basic message delivered at the Unintended Consequences: The Impact of Migration Law and Policy Conference, 25–26 October 2013, The Australian National University, Canberra. In particular, I draw most heavily on some parts of Benjamin Powell and Zachary Gochenour, 'Broken Borders: Government, Foreign-born Workers, and the US Economy' (Policy Report, The Independent Institute, September 2013).
2   OECD, 'Key Indicators on International Migration'. Available at: www.oecd.org/els/mig/ke yindicatorsoninternationalmigration.htm.
3   Julian Simon, *The Ultimate Resource* (Princeton University Press, 1981).

This chapter examines the economic consequences, both intended and unintended, of immigration. Although economic theory will be applied to Australia's circumstances, the general economic case for immigration is also applicable in other developed and relatively economically free countries.

Many objections to greater immigrant flows are grounded in economic fallacies. This chapter proceeds by documenting the basic economics of international trade in labour and examining the merits of three popular economic fallacies: that immigrants harm the economy; steal our jobs; and depress the wages of the native born. Finally, other fiscal, criminal, and political problems are briefly considered.

Immigration's impact on the economy

Contrary to many popular fears,[4] immigrants improve the economic welfare of the native-born population. Free trade in labour, like trade in goods and services, frees Australians and permanent residents to do what is in their comparative advantage. In fact, the basic economic case for free trade in labour is not fundamentally different than that for trade in goods and services.

Trade barriers for goods and services have fallen considerably since the establishment of the General Agreement on Tariffs and Trade (GATT) in 1947. Support for free trade in goods and services commands more consent among economists than virtually any other issue. In fact, free trade has been a core issue for economists ever since Adam Smith's *An Inquiry into the Nature and Causes of the Wealth of Nations* (1776).

The basic case for free trade builds on the fact that different people in different places have different abilities to produce goods and services. If governments allow them to trade freely, market forces will naturally push each person (and country) to produce those goods and services that they can produce at the lowest cost and import those goods and

---

4   CNN correspondent Lou Dobbs is a prime example of the types of fears held by many in the general public. See 'Lou Dobbs calls economists "jackasses"', www.youtube.com/watch?v=zoDb3D7B2Zo.

services that they could only produce at greater expense. As a result, market exchange creates more wealth than would be created in the absence of such exchange.[5]

Substitute labour mobility for the mobility of goods and services, and the process works in the same way. Given their abilities, interests, and costs, each labourer moves to where he can create relatively more value for others. If capital, natural resources, and goods and services were all perfectly mobile, labour mobility wouldn't be as economically important as it is.

But barriers to trade in goods and capital flows remain; some services must be provided in person, and, by definition, many natural resources are in a fixed geographical location. Thus, labour mobility remains crucial for our prosperity. In fact, the benefits of increasing labour mobility greatly dwarfs the gains that could be achieved through further removal of barriers to capital flows and trade in goods and services.

Economist Michael Clemens has documented that completely eliminating global barriers to immigration would result in net gains of $30 to $90 trillion for the world's economy (50 to 150 per cent of world GDP).[6] Even a smaller migration of 5 per cent of people from poorer parts to wealthier parts of the world would result in wealth gains that exceed those that could be had by eliminating remaining trade and capital flow barriers.

Of course, many of the benefits Clemens estimates would go to the immigrants themselves. What about the net benefit of immigration to the native-born population? Harvard economist George Borjas is probably the most widely known academic critic of unfettered immigration, but even he admits that immigrants create net benefits for the native-born and, in the *Concise Encyclopedia of Economics*,

---

5   David Ricardo, *On the Principles of Political Economy and Taxation* (Cambridge University Press, 1817).
6   Michael Clemens, 'Economics and Emigration: Trillion-Dollar Bills on the Sidewalk? (2011) 25 *Journal of Economic Perspectives* 83.

he puts this gain at $22 billion a year in the United States.[7] Applying this same methodology to Australia results in an estimated net benefit for the native-born population of $9 billion.[8]

Relative to the $1.5 trillion Australian economy, $9 billion is a modest 0.6 per cent of GDP. Other methods of calculating the net benefits of immigration lead to larger numbers, though all remain modest as a percentage of the economy.[9] However, it is important to keep in mind that the current level of benefits natives derive from immigration is related directly to the Australian Government's restrictive immigration policies. Obviously, more immigrants would increase the gains. Current policy also dictates that some migrants, including refugees, are ineligible to participate in the labour force. Even so, the important point is that economists have a wide agreement that immigration, like free trade, brings net benefits to the existing native-born population.[10] Thus a smaller economy and lower standard of living are one of the unintended and undesirable consequences of restrictive immigration policies.

Immigrants do not take jobs from the native born

That immigrants take our jobs is probably the most repeated and most economically ignorant objection to immigration. It is a classic example of Bastiat's 'broken window fallacy' ('what is seen and what is not seen').[11] Everyone can see when an immigrant takes a job that was

---

7   George Borjas, 'Immigration' in David R Henderson (ed.), *The Concise Encyclopedia of Economics* (Liberty Fund, 2009) 253.

8   Calculated as GDP multiplied by $1/2sem2$ where s = labour's share of GDP, e = the elasticity of labour demand with respect to the wage, and m = the fraction of the labour force that is foreign born.

9   See George Borjas, above fn 7, for some references to alternative methodologies.

10   See the Independent Institute's Open Letter on Immigration, its signatories, and the references at the end of the letter for evidence of this consensus. Alexander Tabarrok and David Theroux, 'Open Letter on Immigration', *Independent Institute*, 19 June 2006. Available at: www.independent.org/newsroom/article.asp?id=1727.

11   Frédéric Bastiat, 'What Is Seen and What Is Not Seen' in George B. de Huszar (ed.) Seymour Cain (trans.), *Selected Essays on Political Economy* (Foundation for Economic Education, 1848). In Bastiat's example, a window is broken and people erroneously believe that the town will become wealthier because now someone must be paid to replace it. They overlook the unseen fact that the money would have been spent elsewhere in the economy if the window had not been broken.

held by a native-born worker. But not everyone sees the secondary consequence of the new jobs that are created because native-born labour has been freed up for more productive uses. In the market's process of creative destruction, jobs are created and destroyed all the time.

If, on balance, immigrants really did take jobs from existing native-born workers without new jobs being created, the same should be true any time we add more workers to the economy. As Figure 6.1 shows, the Australian civilian labour force has nearly doubled since 1978.[12] Yet there has been no long-term increase in the unemployment rate. In 1978, the unemployment rate was 6.3 per cent,[13] and currently it is 5.7 per cent.[14] As more people enter the labour force, more people get jobs.

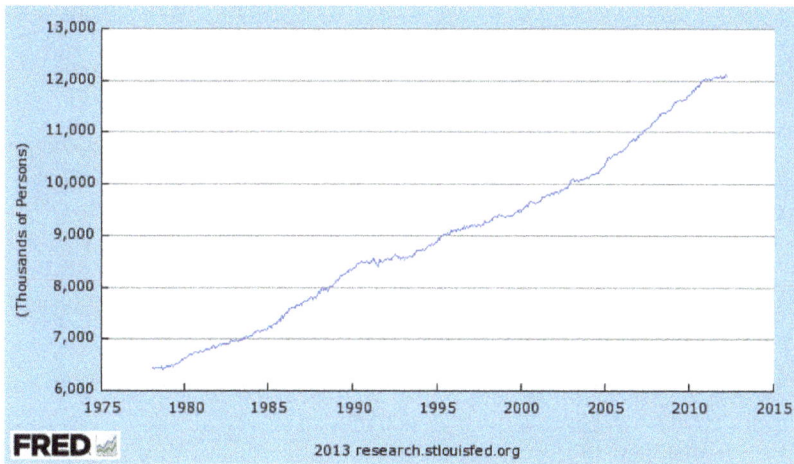

Figure 6.1: Civilian labour force: All persons in Australia.
Source: Organisation for Economic Co-operation and Development.

---

12   The civilian labour force includes all non-military people employed or seeking employment in Australia.

13   Trading Economics, 'Australia's Unemployment Rate', (7 November 2013). Available at: www.tradingeconomics.com/australia/unemployment-rate.

14   Australia Bureau of Statistics, *Labour Force, Australia, Oct 2013* (7 November 2013). Available at: www.abs.gov.au/ausstats/abs@.nsf/mf/6202.0.

Immigration advocates often argue that immigrants do the jobs Australians won't do. Critics of immigration often reply that if wages for these jobs were higher, Australians would be more willing to do them. However, this reply overlooks the fact that if wages were higher, many of the jobs simply wouldn't exist. For example, in the United States approximately one-third of all garment workers are immigrants. If wages needed to be higher to get Australians to take the jobs, many of these jobs would have gone overseas. Examples abound of farmers in the United States deciding that it was better not to produce than to pay higher wages. In Arizona, for example, only 30 per cent of the 2004 lettuce crop was harvested; the rest was left in the ground to rot. Losses amounted to nearly US$1 billion. Farmers certainly could have paid higher wages to get the crop harvested, but the losses would presumably have been even greater.

Immigrants don't depress wage rates

This leads to the third most common economic objection to immigration. Any student who has taken an introductory economics course would think, quite plausibly, that if the supply of labour increases, more workers will be employed, but the wage rate will fall. The first part is true: as noted above, more workers are employed. However, the second part is not: wage rates do not necessarily fall. A survey of the economics literature on immigration concluded that '[d]espite the popular belief that immigrants have a large adverse impact on the wages and employment opportunities of the native born population, the literature on this question does not provide much support for the conclusion'.[15]

More research has been done since that survey was written, but the general conclusions remain much the same.[16] Economists find no evidence of widespread declines in real wages. The debate on the

---

15   Rachel Friedberg and Jennifer Hunt, 'The Impact of Immigrants on Host Country Wages, Employment and Growth' (1995) 9 *Journal of Economic Perspectives* 23.
16   Sari Pekkala Kerr and William R Kerr, 'Economic Impacts of Immigration: A Survey' (NBER Working Paper 16736, 2011).

effect of immigration on wage rates of native-born workers has mostly narrowed to the effect on wages of high-school drop-outs.[17] Estimates range from slightly positive to, at worst, an 8 per cent fall.[18]

How is this possible? Don't the laws of supply and demand dictate that wages would fall? Not when other things change at the same time. Those immigrants who add to the supply of labour also demand goods and services, causing the demand for labour to rise. This means that the effect of immigration on wages shifts from being a theoretical question to being an empirical one. Figure 6.2 illustrates the three possible theoretical outcomes.

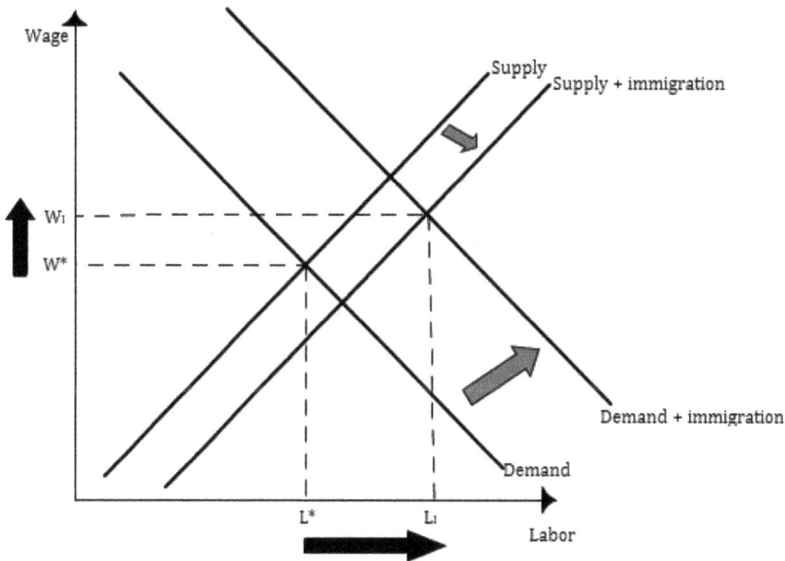

Figure 6.2a: Demand shift magnitude > supply shift magnitude.
Source: Author's research.

---

17   For a couple of classic examples in the conflicting sides of that debate, see George Borjas, 'The Labor Demand Curve is Downward Sloping: Reexamining the Impact of Immigration on the Labor Market' (2003) 118 *Quarterly Journal of Economics* 1335; David Card and Andrei Shleifer, 'Immigration and Inequality' (2009) 99 *Australian Economic Review* 1.
18   See Independent Institute's open letter, above fn 10, for references.

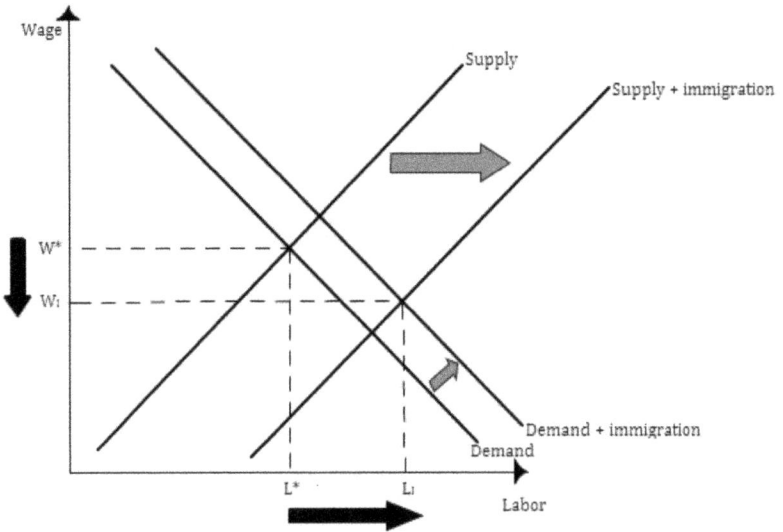

Figure 6.2b: Supply shift magnitude > demand shift magnitude.
Source: Author's research.

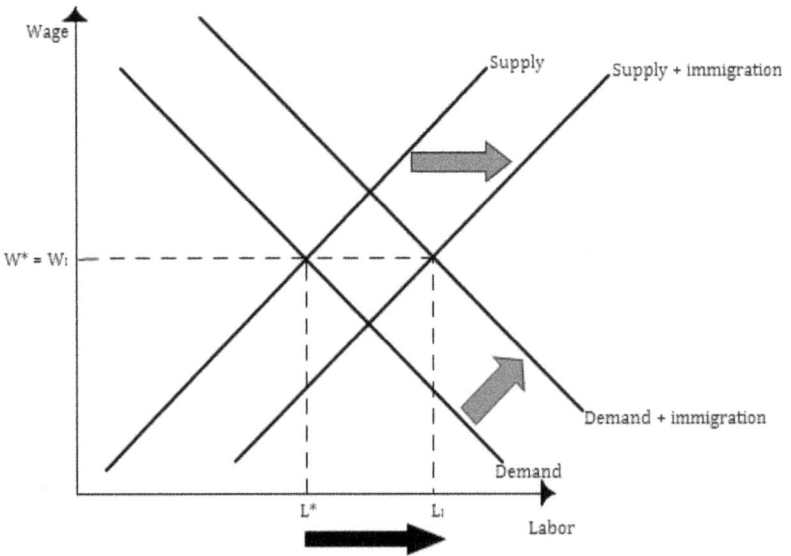

Figure 6.2c: Demand shift magnitude > supply shift magnitude.
Source: Author's research.

In the first panel (Figure 6.2a) the demand for goods and services by immigrants is greater than the amount they increase the supply of labour, and wages rise. In the second panel (Figure 6.2b) their demand for goods and services is less than they increase the supply of labour, and wages fall. In the final panel (Figure 6.2c) immigrants' demand for goods and services are proportional to the increase in the supply of labour, and wages remain unchanged. Which of these three panels describes any particular country's experience is an empirical matter, not a theoretical one.

Second, immigrants don't simply shift the supply of labour. Labour is heterogeneous. When immigrants have skills that differ from those of the native born population, they complement the native born rather than serving as substitutes for them. Many immigrants are either extremely highly skilled or very low-skilled.[19] Yet most native-born labour falls somewhere in between. To the extent that immigrants are complementing domestic labour, they can increase, rather than reduce, the wages of the native-born.

Third, even for the unskilled, the issue of price sensitivity needs to be taken into account. If the demand for workers is perfectly elastic in the relevant range, then there need not be any effect on wages.[20] Finally, as Adam Smith pointed out centuries ago, specialisation and the division of labour are limited by the extent of the market. Bringing more immigrants into Australia expands the market and allows for greater specialisation. That makes each of us more productive and able to earn higher wages. This effect is particularly important in a country that is as large and yet sparsely populated as Australia.

Fiscal impact of immigrants

Another common fear is that immigrants are a fiscal drain on the government's budget. Some people might legitimately fear that changes to immigration policy would drain the federal budget or cause fiscal deficits. But because net economic gains flow from immigration, any

---

19   Evidence for the United States can be found in Matthew Hall et al., 'The Geography of Immigrant Skills: Educational Profiles of Metropolitan Areas' (Brookings Paper, 2011). Casual empiricism indicates that the same is likely true in Australia.
20   See Bryan Caplan's discussion of the contradiction within David Card's work on this point. Bryan Caplan, 'An Infinite Contradiction', *EconLog*, 19 May 2005. Available at: econlog.econlib. org/archives/2005/05/infinite_contra.html.

budgetary imbalances should be solvable by changes to fiscal policy. Because immigration increases the size of the economic pie, re-cutting the pieces of the pie should be able to address fiscal concerns.

Nobel laureate economist Milton Friedman famously declared: 'You cannot simultaneously have free immigration and a welfare state.'[21] Many people take this to mean that immigration should be limited. However, the obvious alternative is to not allow immigrants access to the programs that comprise today's welfare state, including taxpayer-financed public education and healthcare programs. When Milton Friedman was asked about that alternative he commented: 'I haven't really ever thought of that system.'[22] Luckily, a recent policy study by Alex Nowrasteh and Sophie Cole has considered this alternative system.[23] Nowrasteh and Cole argue for building a wall around the US welfare state rather than a wall around the United States. They specifically suggest eliminating non-citizen access to Temporary Aid to Needy Families, Supplemental Nutrition Assistance Program, Supplemental Social Security Income, and Medicaid. Similar reforms would limit the desire of any future immigrants to come to Australia for access to the Australian welfare state. Of course there could be further unintended consequences of such a policy (see Chapter 4) but surely, at least from a potential immigrant's perspective, the offer of a migration visa without access to the welfare state is a much better deal than no visa at all.

Other concerns about immigration

Not all objections to greater migration are grounded in economic fallacies. It is beyond the scope of this paper to examine every objection to immigration, but there is one worth mentioning very briefly.

Australia has a high standard of living because it has a relatively good underlying economic institutional environment. An overwhelming scholarly literature has shown that greater economic freedom and a better security of private property rights cause higher standards

---

21   Peter Brimelow and Milton Friedman, 'Milton Friedman Soothsayer' (1998) 2 *Hoover Digest*.
22   Q&A session with Milton Friedman at the 18th Annual Institute for Liberty and Policy Analysis (ISIL) World Libertarian Conference, 20–22 August 1999, San Jose, Costa Rica.
23   Sophie Cole and Alex Nowrasteh, 'Building a Wall Around the Welfare State, Instead of the Country' (Cato Policy Analysis 732, July 2013).

of living and greater rates of economic growth.[24] It is precisely this environment of economic freedom that makes immigration so economically beneficial. The 'Economic Freedom of the World Annual Report' is the best available measure of this environment. Australia currently ranks as the fifth freest economy in the world.[25] Over the last 30 years Australia has never ranked below being the thirteenth freest economy.

One might fear that new immigrants will change the political environment and undermine political support for economic freedom, thus lowering the living standards of the native-born. Although possible, I think there are strong reasons to be sceptical of this fear. It is usually raised in the context of poorer, less skilled immigrants and refugees. But these immigrants overwhelmingly come from countries with much less economic freedom, and it is that environment that they are fleeing. It seems unlikely that refugees will want to transform Australia's institutions into those of the countries that they recently fled. More likely, as they assimilate into Australia's culture they will also assimilate Australian political ideology. My own recent research is the first to empirically investigate the topic.[26] My co-authors and I examined how immigration impacted economic freedom in 110 countries from 1990 to the present. We find a small but positive increase in economic freedom caused by immigration while controlling for other factors.

Conclusion

The sorting mechanism that is best fitted for finding where immigrants should locate and what they should produce is the free market. In that setting, individuals and businesses contract voluntarily and wage rates balance against the cost of living, providing incentives to distribute the workforce efficiently, geographically and by sector. When labour mobility and wages are tightly controlled, shortages are the likely result.

---

24 See Joshua Hall and Robert A Lawson (eds), *Economic Freedom: Causes and Consequences* (Nova Science Publishers, 2011); Benjamin Powell, *Making Poor Nations Rich: Entrepreneurship and the Process of Development* (Stanford University Press, 2008).
25 James Gwartney, Robert Lawson and Joshua Hall, 'Economic Freedom of the World: 2013 Annual Report' (Fraser Institute).
26 J R Clark et al., 'Does Immigration Impact Economic Freedom?' (CATO Working Paper, 2014).

It is important to consider the question of whether policy-makers could possibly know the right or optimal quota level. Knowledge of labour market conditions is dispersed throughout the economy, and government planners do not know the specific circumstances of time and place as well as entrepreneurs and workers on the spot.[27] Central planning of economic activity has a dismal track record, and the labour market is not fundamentally different from other markets that are impossible to plan. Market conditions are changing constantly, and any quota that might seem appropriate for one time and place will not work in another. The prices and quantities of labour, like other goods and services, need to be continually discovered anew by decentralised bidding between workers and employers. Absent this process, no one knows the right quantity of labour in any given sector.

Eliminating immigration barriers to skilled workers from other wealthy countries should be the least controversial policy change. Much like Australians choosing to migrate between states, there appears to be little concern amongst the public and policy-makers that high-skill immigrants will come for welfare benefits, be criminals, or undermine political institutions. As a policy tool, this cohort presents an easy demographic for governments to encourage. They have high skills and most people understand the ways that they can benefit the Australian economy.

But immigration restrictions on low-skilled workers from poorer countries should also be eliminated. These workers are not an economic burden upon the native-born. The greatest welfare gains for the world economy come from admitting these workers. These workers free up time for more highly skilled Australians to perform other valuable services and do not systematically depress the wages of the native-born. Even if they are a fiscal drain, the appropriate response is to allow them entry and to rearrange fiscal policy so that they cease to be a drain. Because they increase the size of the economic pie, any fiscal drain is a result of poor policy, not an inherent necessity of low-skilled immigration. There is little evidence to suggest that these immigrants do anything to undermine the economic institutions that make Australia wealthy. An open immigration policy for all — high-skill and low-skill workers, from rich and poor countries — would make would-be immigrants much better off and make native-born Australians wealthier too.

---

27   F A Hayek, 'The Use of Knowledge in Society' (1945) 35 *American Economic Review* 519.

Bibliography

Australia Bureau of Statistics, *Labour Force, Australia, Oct 2013* (7 November 2013). Available at: www.abs.gov.au/ausstats/abs@. nsf/mf/6202.0

Bastiat, Frédéric, 'What Is Seen and What Is Not Seen' in George B. de Huszar (ed.) Seymour Cain (trans.), *Selected Essays on Political Economy* (Foundation for Economic Education, 1848)

Borjas, George, 'The Labor Demand Curve is Downward Sloping: Reexamining the Impact of Immigration on the Labor Market' (2003) 118 *Quarterly Journal of Economics* 1335

Borjas, George, 'Immigration' in David R Henderson (ed.), *The Concise Encyclopedia of Economics* (Liberty Fund, 2009) 253

Brimelow, Peter and Milton Friedman, 'Milton Friedman Soothsayer' (1998) 2 *Hoover Digest*

Caplan, Bryan, 'An Infinite Contradiction', *EconLog*, 19 May 2005. Available at: econlog.econlib.org/archives/2005/05/infinite_contra. html

Card, David and Andrei Shleifer, 'Immigration and Inequality' (2009) 99 *Australian Economic Review* 1

Clark, J R, Robert A Lawson, Alex Nowrasteh, Benjamin Powell and Ryan Murphy, 'Does Immigration Impact Economic Freedom?' (CATO Working Paper, 2014)

Clemens, Michael, 'Economics and Emigration: Trillion-Dollar Bills on the Sidewalk?' (2011) 25 *Journal of Economic Perspectives* 83

Cole, Sophie and Alex Nowrasteh, 'Building a Wall Around the Welfare State, Instead of the Country' (Cato Policy Analysis 732, July 2013)

Friedberg, Rachel and Jennifer Hunt, 'The Impact of Immigrants on Host Country Wages, Employment and Growth' (1995) 9 *Journal of Economic Perspectives* 23

Gwartney, James, Robert Lawson and Joshua Hall, 'Economic Freedom of the World: 2013 Annual Report' (Fraser Institute)

Hall, Joshua and Robert A Lawson (eds), *Economic Freedom: Causes and Consequences* (Nova Science Publishers, 2011)

Hall, Matthew, Audrey Singer, Gordon F De Jong and Deborah Roempke Graefe, 'The Geography of Immigrant Skills: Educational Profiles of Metropolitan Areas' (Brookings Paper, 2011)

Hayek, F A, 'The Use of Knowledge in Society' (1945) 35 *American Economic Review* 519

Organisation for Economic Co-operation and Development, *Civilian Labor Force: All Persons in Australia* © [AUSLFTOTADSMEI] (2012). Available from: ALFRED, Federal Reserve Bank of St Louis alfred.stlouisfed.org/series?seid=AUSLFTOTADSMEI

Organisation for Economic Co-operation and Development, 'Key Indicators on International Migration'. Available at: www.oecd.org/els/mig/keyindicatorsoninternationalmigration.htm

Pekkala Kerr, Sari and William R Kerr, 'Economic Impacts of Immigration: A Survey' (NBER Working Paper 16736, 2011)

Powell, Benjamin, *Making Poor Nations Rich: Entrepreneurship and the Process of Development* (Stanford University Press, 2008)

Powell, Benjamin and Zachary Gochenour, 'Broken Borders: Government, Foreign-born Workers, and the US Economy' (Policy Report, The Independent Institute, September 2013)

Ricardo, David, *On the Principles of Political Economy and Taxation* (Cambridge University Press, 1817)

Simon, Julian, *The Ultimate Resource* (Princeton University Press, 1981)

Smith, Adam, *An Inquiry into the Nature and Causes of the Wealth of Nations* (W Strahan and T Cadell, 1776)

Tabarrok, Alexander and David Theroux, 'Open Letter on Immigration', *Independent Institute*, 19 June 2006. Available at: www.independent.org/newsroom/article.asp?id=1727

Trading Economics, 'Australia's Unemployment Rate', 7 November 2013). Available at: www.tradingeconomics.com/australia/unemployment-rate

7

Not Drowning, Waving: Images, History, and the Representation of Asylum Seekers

Desmond Manderson

Since Jeremy Bentham 200 years ago, the concept of law in the developed world has been dominated by a thoroughgoing consequentialism. The purpose of the law, according to Bentham and all those who follow in his footsteps, can be summed up in a single word: utility. Law is thought of not as a symbolic or normative structure so much as a system that causes changes in behaviour by instilling pain or pleasure. This consequentialist logic is based on the assumption that we know, by and large, what effects flow from what causes and can therefore accurately calibrate the consequences on behaviour of any particular legal change. Our actions are intentional and their consequences are predictable. Of course, this is precisely the arrogance behind such a philosophy. Migration law provides a rich tapestry to demonstrate the ways in which our legal intentions and actions bear many, and often gravely counter-productive, fruit. The pages of this volume are devoted to demonstrating the futility, paradox, or irony of a more complex relationship between intention and consequence.

Figure 7.1: 'If you come here by boat'.
Source: Department of Immigration and Citizenship, 2013.

The fate of the Special Humanitarian Program in Australia offers a brief example. As maritime arrivals have increased since 2007, the government has cut back the number of other humanitarian placements we accept by a corresponding amount, notably preventing Australian residents from bringing in family members facing human rights abuse abroad.[1] This linkage had no discernible impact on the number of maritime arrivals. But it has had unintended consequences. In 1999, when a similar linkage policy was introduced, children made up only 13 per cent of asylum seekers. By 2001, faced with the risk of never being able to bring their families out, the proportion of children on boats had risen to one-third.[23] In October 2001, SIEV-X, an 'illegal entry vehicle', sank en route to Christmas Island, claiming the lives of 353 people. Over 40 per cent were women; over 40 per cent were children.[4] Since August 2012, the Australian Government has once again denied anyone arriving in Australia on a temporary visa any right to access the split family program.[5] This particular pain, inutile and destructive, will fall in particular on unaccompanied minors, the most vulnerable of all refugee groups, who face a life indefinitely separated from their parents.

But there is another way of approaching the question of unintended consequences. Let us reject the logic that assumes that all regulation is based on *intention*. Human attitudes are driven by many underlying beliefs, including our fears, anxieties, and assumptions. We might call these unarticulated drivers of behaviour 'ideology'. Perhaps, as Jacques Lacan suggested, we might even say that the unconscious is the government — a body whose obscure decisions we do not know and whose motivations are kept hidden from us, but which nevertheless produces consequences that influence our behaviour. In the sense of ideology or unconscious motivation, most consequences are unintended. Indeed, it is the *fact that they are unintended,* and unavailable to scrutiny, that is the very source of their power.

1   Refugee Council of Australia, *National and Global Statistics 2013–14,* 4. Available at www. refugeecouncil.org.au/r/isub/2013-14-IntakeSub-stat.pdf; Department of Immigration and Citizenship, *Fact Sheet 60.* Available at: www.border.gov.au.virtual.anu.edu.au/about/corporate/information/fact-sheets/60refugee; Janet Phillips, 'Asylum Seekers and Refugees: What are the Facts?' *Parliamentary Library Background Note.* Available at: parlinfo.aph.gov.au/parlInfo/search/display/display.w3p;query=Id%3A%22library%2Fprspub%2FHGNW6%22.
2   Mary Crock and D Ghezelbash, 'Do Loose Lips Bring Ships?: The Role of Policy, Politics and Human Rights in Managing Unauthorised Boat Arrivals' (2010) 19 *Griffith Law Review* 238, 262.
3   Senate Legal and Constitutional Affairs Legislation Committee, *Immigration and Citizenship Portfolio, Supplementary Budget Estimates* (Parliament of Australia, 17 October 2011).
4   Marg Hutton, *Drownings on the Public Record of People Attempting to Enter Australia Irregularly by Boat Since 1998* (2014). Available at: www.sievx.com/articles/background/DrowningsTable.pdf; Tony Kevin, *Reluctant Rescuers* (Union Offset, 2012) 143.
5   Department of Immigration and Citizenship, *Humanitarian Program Information Paper 2013–14,* 3–4; Chris Bowen, 'Government Implements Expert Panel's Family Reunion recommendation' (Media Release, 22 September 2012).

So where might we find the ideological assumptions that create a whole unintended worldview? Not, to be sure, in the explicit words of legal regulation; they are far too self-conscious and explicit for that. Not even in the work of the spin-doctors and commentariat, whose words are devised to justify and modify changes in attitude. Ideology — our unconscious government — sits below the level of justification, at the level of perspective or 'common sense'. It just *is*. We will instead find this framework of meaning not in texts but in images, and in the feelings and responses they evoke. It is these images that shape our response, unbeknownst to us. These images frame how we perceive asylum seekers and govern how we treat them. The whole sorry story of contemporary migration law is but a litany of their unintended consequences. As John Tagg explains it, the image reveals not the logic of an event but the underlying ideology of life's illusions that governs its reception:

> What lies 'behind' the paper or 'behind' the image is not reality — the referent — but reference: a subtle web of discourse through which realism is enmeshed … a whole hidden corpus of knowledge, a social knowledge that is called upon through the mechanism of connotation.[6]

In images we will find clues to the attitudes that influence our response to refugees, and whose consequences, powerful precisely because they operate below intention, we see all around us.

The immigration department's most recent advertising campaign shows a rickety boat in a vast empty ocean. Across the picture are emblazoned the words: 'If you come here in a boat without a visa — YOU WON'T BE SETTLED IN AUSTRALIA'.[7] A similar image is on the department's own website, under the heading 'NO WAY'.[8] The image evokes the loneliness and the dangers of undertaking a sea voyage in which over a thousand people have drowned in the past decade.[9] But it does nothing to tell us about the lives of those on board,

6   John Tagg, *The Burden of Representation: Essays on Photographies and Histories* (University of Massachusetts Press, 1988) 100.

7   Alana Lentin, 'Refugees: A Call for Open Borders and Free Movement for All', *The Guardian*, 23 July 2013. Available at: www.theguardian.com/commentisfree/2013/jul/23/open-borders-australia-asylum-seekers.

8   Australian Customs and Border Protection, *Counter People Smuggling Communication*. Available at: www.customs.gov.au/site/offshore-communication-campaign-people-smuggling.asp. ACBPS and DIBP will be merged from 1 July 2015, however, ACBPS was not a part of the department at the time this chapter was written.

9   Marg Hutton, above fn 4.

and why they have felt compelled to take the dangerous steps they have. Asylum seekers are presented as generic and faceless. While they are worthy of our pity, they are not worthy of our respect.

The same could be said of the coverage of the repatriation of the drowned body of an infant when — yet another — boat sank off Christmas Island in July 2013. Beneath a headline that declared, 'Final journey for policy failure's littlest victim', the iconic image showed the coffin of a 10-week-old boy being loaded into a cargo plane.[10] The image again combines two key elements in the visual discourse of 'irregular maritime arrivals' in Australia: the victim, who is powerless to avert their fate, the plaything of evil predators (and perhaps of their parents' foolishness); and the Australian rescuer who tries to help but is overwhelmed by sheer numbers. Again, what is lacking is any sense of the actual histories of this child's family or others on board the vessel, not to mention the specific circumstances in which taking to the open ocean was a tragic, but by no means an irrational, decision.[11] The image congratulates us on our sense of pity — our own capacity for moral empathy — but does not in any way make us feel implicated in its awful chain of events.

In that light, the harshness of Australia's policies becomes a *righteous* response. Images of detention facilities in places such as Nauru and Manus Island are likewise carefully managed. They keep the viewer at a distance, and show asylum seekers behind barbed wire fences. We are invited to feel a shudder of sublime horror at this fate, but we are never brought close enough to see faces, or engage with individual stories. This specificity might change our relationship to these images, and more to the point we might be brought from a generalised pity of the *circumstances* of these refugees, to anger at the injustice of our own policies. While barbed wire enclosures, like the open ocean,

---

10   Paige Taylor, 'Final Journey for Policy Failure's Littlest Victim', *The Australian*, 29 July 2013. Available at: www.theaustralian.com.au/national-affairs/election-2013/final-journey-for-policy-failures-littlest-victim/story-fn9qr68y-1226687209428.

11   For a comprehensive discussion of the asylum question in Australian law and policy, see Desmond Manderson, 'From Zero Tolerance to Harm Reduction: "The Asylum Problem Problem"' (2013) 32(4) *Refugee Survey Quarterly* 1; Desmond Manderson, 'Groundhog Day: Why the Asylum Problem is Like the Drug Problem' (2013) 41 *Griffith Law Review* 84. See also M Crock, B Saul and A Dastyari, *Future Seekers II: Refugees and Irregular Migration in Australia* (Federation Press, 2006).

are treated as the law of nature, and asylum seekers as something like wild animals at the mercy of those laws, what we are really invited to experience is our own feelings and our own moral virtue.[12]

To understand exactly how these images operate and with what social and legal effects, it can sometimes help to think about a different image from a different time. By doing this, we can take a dispassionate look at the way images work in framing our responses.[13] Take a famous picture from the nineteenth century, J M W Turner's *The Slave Ship* (1840).[14] The painting is a bravura depiction of sunset and seascape.

Most extraordinary is its subject, given in Turner's original title, *Slavers throwing overboard the dead and dying — typhoon coming on.* In the foreground, dwarfed by the fury of the sea and obscured by the glare of the sun, are several tiny figures, hands outstretched in futile appeal as they sink beneath the waves, surrounded by the chains of their bondage. On the right, an even more macabre scene plays out, the dead body of a woman already being devoured by fishes as a great shark bears down.

The picture has a specific legal context. In 1781, 132 captive men and women aboard the *Zong* drowned en route from Africa to the slave markets of the Caribbean. The crew had been ordered by the captain to throw them overboard, so that the ship's owners could claim under an insurance contract that was payable for 'cargo' lost or jettisoned at sea — but not if they died of illness or malnutrition either at sea or after landfall.[15] Turner's point was not merely of historical interest. Britain had only prohibited slavery in its Caribbean colonies two years previously. In 1840, the question of global abolition was hotly debated and the problem of jettison had not gone away.[16] Turner's image

---

12 Sherene Razack, *Dark Threats and White Knights: The Somalia Affair, Peacekeeping, and the New Imperialism* (University of Toronto Press, 2004).

13 W J T Mitchell (ed.), *Art and the Public Sphere* (University of Chicago Press, 1992); W J T Mitchell, *Picture Theory: Essays on Verbal and Visual Representation* (University of Chicago Press, 1994); W J T Mitchell, *What do Pictures Want?: The Lives and Loves of Images* (Chicago University Press, 2005); David Freedberg, *The Power of Images: Studies in the History and Theory of Response* (University of Chicago Press, 1989).

14 Joseph Turner, *The Slave Ship* (*Slavers throwing overboard the dead and dying — typhoon coming on*), oil on canvas, 90.8 x 122.6 cm, Museum of Fine Arts, Boston (1840).

15 *Gregson v Gilbert* (1783) 99 ER 629; John McCoubrey, 'Turner's Slave Ship: Abolition, Ruskin, and Reception' (1998) 14(4) *Word and Image* 319.

16 See, for example, *Spectator*, 'Debates and Proceedings in Parliament. Amendment of the Slave Emancipation Act', 17 March 1838, p. 2.

reminded his viewers of an historical tragedy in order to draw attention to a current issue. It represented the ills of slavery and appealed for the completion of a job half done.[17]

The Slave Ship is probably Turner's most controversial painting. For some critics, it is a stirring indictment of a dark chapter in British history. In these images of death and drowning, we are brought closer to the callous horror of the slave trade. Some have gone further, suggesting that his real subject was not just slavery, but the cold logic of capitalism that reduced human beings to a matter of costs and benefits. The poem that Turner wrote to accompany the painting suggests as much: 'Hope, Hope, fallacious hope/Where is thy market now?' The slaver, the shark, and the capitalist all feast on human flesh.[18]

Other critics vehemently disagree. Many find Turner's painting grotesque and melodramatic. The human figures lack individuality, personality, or history. We do not see their eyes, we do not see their faces. He treats them like animals in death, just as they had been treated in life. The dead and drowning are abject — presented as objects for whom we feel pity, not as subjects to whom we owe respect. Even worse, by turning them into an artwork notable for its gorgeous and subtle colours, is he not exploiting their suffering for his own purposes?[19] The debate over the meaning of *The Slave Ship* comes down to whether such images and events can — and should — be represented in art. Does aesthetic portrayal deepen the impact of their suffering, or merely appropriate it for our amusement? It is not an easy question. It is true that there is a maudlin tendency in Turner's depiction of the victims of slavery. They are presented as a group, doomed by nature to suffering, rather than as individuals with perspectives of their own. They are reduced to mere bodies without history or agency. Such an abject portrayal objectifies human beings in a disturbing way: it seems to take from them their dignity. But at the

---

17 See Paul Gilroy, *The Black Atlantic* (Cambridge University Press, 1993); Marcus Wood, *Blind Memory: Visual Representations of Slavery in England and America, 1780–1865* (Manchester Press, 2000).
18 Jerrold Ziff, 'John Langhorne and Turner's "Fallacies of Hope"' (1964) 27 *Journal of Warburg and Courtauld Institutes* 340.
19 See Paul Gilroy, *The Black Atlantic* (Cambridge University Press, 1993); Abigail Ward, '"Words are all I have left of my eyes": Blinded by the Past in J. M. W. Turner's *Slavers Throwing Overboard the Dead and Dying* and David Dabydeen's "Turner"' (2007) 42 *The Journal of Commonwealth Literature* 47.

same time, Turner emphasises an uncomfortable truth about human existence. To look at the painting is to confront one's own mortality. The loss of dignity and the abrogation of rights comes to us all in the end — in death if not in old age, in old age if not in sickness, in sickness if not in childhood, in childhood if not in birth, in birth if not in sex, in love and in death. This does not remove the question of others' responsibility. On the contrary, it heightens it. In death we are *all* reduced to the forces of nature, to a lifeless and right-less corpse whose treatment matters just because there is nothing and no one to demand it, except the scruples of those who survive.

Indeed, the disagreement over Turner's painting is a false dichotomy. *The Slave Ship* depicts both a moral feeling *and* a moral failing. It represents a system of exploitation — the basis of British prosperity in the eighteenth century — that the Empire was ultimately prepared to recognise and to reject. But it also represents a system of exploitation — the basis of British prosperity in the nineteenth century — that the Empire was not prepared to acknowledge. By representing black people as passive victims, and failing to imagine their capacity for agency, individuality, and history, Turner's painting expresses the moral complacency that actively produced the Empire. The 'white man's burden', as Kipling would call it, presumed that dark-skinned people had to be dragged like unwilling flotsam from the waters of their destiny:

> To wait in heavy harness
> On fluttered folk and wild —
> Your new-caught, sullen peoples,
> Half devil and half child.[20]

So the brilliance of Turner's masterpiece lies in his ability to intentionally reveal the story of British slavery, while at the same time unintentionally revealing the mindset of British colonialism. This is what makes many works of art great: they show more than they know. We are always in the presence of not one but *two* perspectives: the object that is pictured and the gaze that pictures it. In this way, Turner succeeds in illuminating both the insight *and* the blindness of the nineteenth-century world view.

---

20   Rudyard Kipling and Thomas James Wise, *The White Man's Burden* (1899); Rudyard Kipling and R T Jones (eds), *The Collected Poems of Rudyard Kipling* (Wordsworth Editions Limited, 1994). See also Sherene Razack above fn 12.

The questions Turner's painting raises, of economic calculation versus human dignity — alive or dead — have not gone away. In June 2013, at least 55 Tamil asylum seekers drowned off Christmas Island. Although an extensive search and rescue operation found no survivors, several dead bodies were located, but never recovered. Border Protection authorities described the decision as 'operational' and claimed that its vessels were needed elsewhere.[21]

With at least three vessels and five aircraft involved in a three-day search, it seems unlikely that Customs had no resources to collect the dead if they had chosen to do so. As the head of the Australian Tamil Congress, Bala Vigneswaran said: 'If the Government, or the decision-makers, think it is OK to leave the people behind because they are not Australian and they're not worth it — if they want to put it that way — it's not right.'[22]

To leave dead bodies in the water, just because it is more convenient to do so, smacks of the kind of instrumental calculation that Turner saw in the story of the slave ship. Yet without an image, without a picture of death as it found those individual lives, the reality is, in some ways, too easy to push into the background of our minds. We are prepared to pity them, of course, in the abstract, as a statistical number of deaths at sea; we are prepared to blame them, even, for the misguided risks they took; what we are not prepared to do is imagine them as people who even in death have families and communities that cherish their bodies and their memories.

At the same time, the other side of Turner's image has its counterpart in contemporary images. The images of asylum seekers with which we are surrounded exploit the same relationships of victimhood, pity, and moral complacency that many critics saw in Turner's canvas. Positioning asylum seekers as victims in the thrall of natural or social forces beyond our control, and ourselves as their well-intentioned but overwhelmed rescuers, blinds us to other questions and perspectives. I mean, for example, the global political structure that treats asylum seeking as a national problem of border control, rather than a regional problem of human security. Or, again, the underlying global economic

21   Judith Ireland, 'Bodies of Drowned Asylum Seekers Left in the Water', *Sydney Morning Herald*, 9 June 2013. Available at: www.smh.com.au/federal-politics/political-news/bodies-of-drowned-asylum-seekers-left-in-the-water-20130609-2ny85.html.
22   Ibid.

structures that assume that capital must be globally free but labour must be tightly controlled. The sincerity of politicians who cry in parliament during debates over the deaths of asylum seekers at sea may do them credit.[23] But perhaps the lure of pity is that if we see ourselves as rescuers and bystanders, in the end the ones we feel sorriest for are ourselves.

Above all, the images with which I started represent boat arrivals as distant victims and obsess only about how to turn them back. This erases the ways in which we are *already* implicated in their lives and choices. Refugees are driven out of their own countries by a political instability that we are not wholly innocent of, or by wars in which we have been actively involved. They are also driven to our shores by desires — for wealth, for capitalism, for commodities — that we encourage and need, and by poverty — cheap labour, cheap goods — that we are more than keen to exploit.[24] The brutality of sweatshops and the tyranny of debt in the developing world is part of the global division of labour. Slavery might be thought of as a system that built a high standard of living for some, while choosing to ignore its dependence on the exploitation of others. Colonialism moved this relationship offshore, where it became more prevalent — and less visible. Post-colonialism merely disguises more effectively still the logic of the process behind the fig-leaf of self-government.

Indeed, if we return to the image of *The Slave Ship* one more time, some odd features are worthy of note. One, that has frequently invited derision, is the way that Turner seems to have painted the heavy iron chains of the slaves as if they were somehow floating on the surface of the water. Another lies in Turner's title, since the picture does not in fact show 'slavers *throwing* overboard the dead and dying'. The ghostly ship lies far off, engulfed by the typhoon, while the dead and dying are right in front of us. Yet there is an answer to these puzzles. What if Turner was right, and the picture actually shows the very moment when they were in the process of being thrown overboard? Then the image would capture the *instant* those chains hit the water — they would not be floating, but they would not yet have sunk.

---

23   News.com.au, 'Tears in Parliament Over Asylum-seeker Deaths at Sea', 27 June 2012. Available at: www.news.com.au/national/tears-in-parliament-over-asylum-seeker-deaths-at-sea/story-e6frfkvr-1226410278096.

24   See Dauvergne, Catherine, *Making People Illegal: What Globalization means for Migration and Law* (Cambridge University Press, 2008).

In that case, however, the ship in the distance cannot be responsible. There must be some *other* ship from which the slavers are throwing the dead and dying. And the solution is simple. We cannot see it because the picture is drawn from its position. *The Slave Ship is us.* If we think of the painting in this way, if we were the slavers all along, then that would surely change our response to those bodies that lie so close to us in the water. We would owe them something, for they would incite not our pity but our responsibility.

That is a bitter pill to swallow. If, as Turner suggests in his image and his title, there is a 'typhoon coming on', a terrible global reckoning, most of us find it hard to admit, and all of us find it hard to do much about it. Nonetheless, Turner's perspectives — the one he could see and the one he couldn't see — are not mutually exclusive. On the contrary, seeing the one is the condition for seeing the other. If Customs had thought of their own families in that water, I cannot but think that they would have acted, urgently and without calculation. And if we had more and better images and stories of those who set out in the 'fallacious hope', as Turner put it, of reaching this country, we would treat them with more respect. Our government and our agencies might even begin to acknowledge the ways in which we are already part of these stories and these lives.

A critical apprehension of the highly emotive images by which we are bombarded will make us much more aware of the ways in which they work on the subconscious to constitute and govern our emotional responses.[25] Such a critical apprehension might also encourage the production of other and different images; showing us, for example, the view of the Australian coast from that rickety boat, or documenting the experiences of those behind the razor wire.[26] Those images already exist, but they do not circulate as often, as reliably, or with the ideological support bestowed on the mainstream images, to which I have alluded in this paper. Nonetheless, even in their relative absence, imagining the framework that has been cut out of the image, so to speak, can still generate a cascade of ironies with powerful effect.[27] The image of a solider bringing back to Australian soil the coffin

---

25   Richard Sherwin, *Visualizing Law in the Age of the Digital Neo-Baroque* (Routledge, 2012); Judith Butler, *Frames of War: When is Life Grievable* (Verso, 2009); John Tagg above fn 6.

26   Ariella Azoulay, *The Civil Contract of Photography* (Zone Books, 2008).

27   John Tagg above fn 6.

of a baby, while his parents and siblings are denied that entry because they are still alive, is just one such irony that can be considered and expounded to show the limitations of our perspective and the consequences of our policies. Visual literacy allows us to reflect on the ways in which images are chosen to enhance particular effects and relationships, and to obfuscate or exclude others. Above all, by allowing us to expand our visual horizons, we may be finally brought to see the responsibility we bear for those who drown at sea — not just in an abstract and sentimental sense, but in an immediate and political sense. Perhaps then our studiously maintained blind spots as to their lives and their deaths would cease.

Bibliography

Articles, books, and reports

Azoulay, Ariella, *The Civil Contract of Photography* (Zone Books, 2008)

Butler, Judith, *Frames of War: When is Life Grievable* (Verso, 2009)

Crock, M, B Saul and A Dastyari, *Future Seekers II: Refugees and Irregular Migration in Australia* (Federation Press, 2006)

Crock, Mary and D Ghezelbash, 'Do Loose Lips Bring Ships?: The Role of Policy, Politics and Human Rights in Managing Unauthorised Boat Arrivals', (2010) 19 *Griffith Law Review* 238

Dauvergne, Catherine, *Making People Illegal: What Globalization means for Migration and Law* (Cambridge University Press, 2008)

Department of Immigration and Citizenship, *Australia's Humanitarian Program 2013–2014*

Freedberg, David, *The Power of Images: Studies in the History and Theory of Response* (University of Chicago Press, 1989)

Gilroy, Paul, *The Black Atlantic* (Cambridge University Press, 1993)

Kevin, Tony, *Reluctant Rescuers* (Union Offset, 2012)

Kipling, Rudyard and R T Jones (eds), *The Collected Poems of Rudyard Kipling* (Wordsworth Editions Limited, 1994)

Kipling, Rudyard and Thomas James Wise, *The White Man's Burden* (1899)

Manderson, Desmond, 'Bodies in the Water' (2013) 264 *Art Monthly Australia* 9

Manderson, Desmond, 'From Zero Tolerance to Harm Reduction: "The Asylum Problem Problem"' (2013) 32(4) *Refugee Survey Quarterly* 1

Manderson, Desmond, 'Groundhog Day: Why the Asylum Problem is Like the Drug Problem' (2013) 41 *Griffith Law Review* 84

McCoubrey, John, 'Turner's Slave Ship: Abolition, Ruskin, and Reception' (1998) 14(4) *Word and Image* 319

Mitchell, W J T (ed.), *Art and the Public Sphere* (University of Chicago Press, 1992)

Mitchell, W J T, *Picture Theory: Essays on Verbal and Visual Representation* (University of Chicago Press, 1994)

Mitchell, W J T, *What do Pictures Want?: The Lives and Loves of Images* (Chicago University Press, 2005)

Razack, Sherene, *Dark Threats and White Knights: The Somalia Affair, Peacekeeping, and the New Imperialism* (University of Toronto Press, 2004)

Senate Legal and Constitutional Affairs Legislation Committee, *Immigration and Citizenship Portfolio, Supplementary Budget Estimates* (Parliament of Australia, 17 October 2011)

Sherwin, Richard, *Visualizing Law in the Age of the Digital Neo-Baroque* (Routledge, 2012)

Spectator, 'Debates and Proceedings in Parliament. Amendment of the Slave Emancipation Act', 17 March 1838, p. 2

Tagg, John, *The Burden of Representation: Essays on Photographies and Histories* (University of Massachusetts Press, 1988)

Ward, Abigail, '"Words are all I have left of my eyes": Blinded by the Past in J. M. W. Turner's Slavers Throwing Overboard the Dead and Dying and David Dabydeen's "Turner"' (2007) 42 *The Journal of Commonwealth Literature* 47

Wood, Marcus, *Blind Memory: Visual Representations of Slavery in England and America, 1780–1865* (Manchester Press, 2000)

Ziff, Jerrold, 'John Langhorne and Turner's "Fallacies of Hope"' (1964) 27 *Journal of Warburg and Courtauld Institutes* 340

Cases

Gregson v Gilbert (1783) 99 ER 629

Other

Australian Customs and Border Protection, *Counter People Smuggling Communication*. Available at: www.customs.gov.au/site/offshore-communication-campaign-people-smuggling.asp

Bowen, Chris, 'Government Implements Expert Panel's Family Reunion recommendation' (Media Release, 22 September 2012)

Department of Immigration and Citizenship, Fact Sheet 60 (2013). Available at: www.border.gov.au.virtual.anu.edu.au/about/corporate/information/fact-sheets/60refugee

Hutton, Marg, *Drownings on the Public Record of People Attempting to Enter Australia Irregularly by Boat Since 1998* (2014). Available at: www.sievx.com/articles/background/DrowningsTable.pdf

Ireland, Judith, 'Bodies of Drowned Asylum Seekers Left in the Water', *Sydney Morning Herald*, 9 June 2013. Available at: www.smh.com.au/federal-politics/political-news/bodies-of-drowned-asylum-seekers-left-in-the-water-20130609-2ny85.html

Lentin, Alana, 'Refugees: A Call for Open Borders and Free Movement for All', *The Guardian*, 23 July 2013. Available at: www.theguardian.com/commentisfree/2013/jul/23/open-borders-australia-asylum-seekers

News.com.au, 'Tears in Parliament Over Asylum-seeker Deaths at Sea', 27 June 2012. Available at: www.news.com.au/national/tears-in-parliament-over-asylum-seeker-deaths-at-sea/story-e6frfkvr-1226410278096

Phillips, Janet, 'Asylum Seekers and Refugees: What are the Facts?' *Parliamentary Library Background Note*. Available at: parlinfo.aph. gov.au/parlInfo/search/display/display.w3p;query=Id%3A%22li brary%2Fprspub%2FHGNW6%22

Refugee Council of Australia, *National and Global Statistics 2013– 14*. Available at: www.refugeecouncil.org.au/r/isub/2013-14-IntakeSub-stat.pdf

Taylor, Paige, 'Final Journey for Policy Failure's Littlest Victim', *The Australian*, 29 July 2013. Available at: www.theaustralian. com.au/national-affairs/election-2013/final-journey-for-policy-failures-littlest-victim/story-fn9qr68y-1226687209428

Turner, Joseph, *The Slave Ship* (Slavers throwing overboard the dead and dying — typhoon coming on), oil on canvas, 90.8 x 122.6 cm, Museum of Fine Arts, Boston (1840)

Notes on Contributors

Marianne Dickie is a senior academic at the Migration Law Program in ANU College of Law. She is passionate about migration law and practice, having worked extensively in the migration field since 1993. Marianne remains determined to improve the legal support system for all migrants by providing future migration agents and legal practitioners the best possible education. Marianne managed the Migration Law Program from 2007–15 as convenor, sub-dean and director. Marianne also understands the importance of grassroots work in this legal space. In 2007, she established a pro bono migration advice clinic that provides support previously unavailable or unaffordable to migrants in the ACT. Her commitment to human rights was recognised in 2012 when she was a finalist for the ACT Australian of the Year. Marianne is a general editor of *Immigration Review*, published by LexisNexis, and a Senior Fellow of the Higher Education Academy. She is a registered migration agent, holds a master's degree in higher education, and is currently completing a doctorate of professional studies focusing on migration agents. She continues to research and write in her two areas of passion: education and migration.

Dorota Anna Gozdecka completed her PhD in legal theory in 2009 at the University of Helsinki, and has recently obtained the title of docent (adjunct professor) of jurisprudence from the same university. Her primary research area focuses on legal theoretical aspects related to the accommodation of cultural diversity. Her recent publications — such as *Identity, Subjectivity and the Access to the Community of Rights,* a special issue of *Social Identities* (2015), the monograph *Rights, Religious Pluralism and the Recognition of Difference: Off the Scales of Justice* (2015), and the edited volume *Europe at the Edge of Pluralism* — explore, in particular, questions of otherness created by contemporary legal regimes. Issues related to the recognition of difference and the place of the other have recently led her to shift her research focus to the area of law and humanities, and to explore the relationship between law and image in the area of migration law. Dorota has previously held research fellowships at the UC Berkeley Institute for European Studies (2013), ANU Centre for European Studies (2012–13), and the European University Institute (2008). She has won prestigious research grants, such as the University of Helsinki three-year grant for an international research project 'Law and the Other', which she is currently leading.

Joanne Kinslor (BA, LLB (Hons) (Sydney)) is a principal solicitor of Kinslor Prince Lawyers, a leading Australian immigration law firm practising in all areas of the complex jurisdiction of Australian immigration and citizenship law, from first instance visa applications through to judicial review. Since 2006 she has been accredited as a specialist in the field of immigration law by the Law Society of New South Wales. Joanne has been recognised in the *Australian Financial Review* as one of Australia's finest immigration lawyers through inclusion in 'Best Lawyers — Australia, Immigration Law' from 2008–16, and was voted Immigration Lawyer of the Year by her peers in 2016. Joanne teaches Australian immigration law and practice at the University of New South Wales as part of the university's law degree program. Joanne is regularly called upon by industry and peak professional bodies to present papers on Australian immigration and citizenship law. She is an affiliate member of the Andrew and Renata Kaldor Centre for International Refugee Law, and is co-creator, contributor, and principal editor of *Immigration Law Review*, which provides an ongoing comprehensive review of legislative amendments and analysis of developments within the field of Australian immigration law.

Desmond Manderson is jointly appointed in the colleges of Law, and Arts and Social Sciences at The Australian National University. He is an international leader in interdisciplinary legal scholarship whose books include *From Mr Sin to Mr Big* (1993), *Songs Without Music: Aesthetic Dimensions of Law and Justice* (2000), *Proximity, Levinas, and the Soul of Law* (2006), and *Kangaroo Courts and the Rule of Law* (2012). After 15 years at McGill University, where he held the Canada Research Chair in Law and Discourse and was foundation Director of the Institute for the Public Life of Arts and Ideas, he returned to Australia in 2012. With the support of an ARC Future Fellowship, his recent work includes *Law and the Visual: Representations, Technologies and Critique* (2016), and *Temporalities of Law in the Visual Arts* (2017).

Peter Mares is an adjunct fellow at the Institute for Social Research at Swinburne University, a contributing editor with the national affairs magazine *Inside Story*, and senior moderator with the Cranlana Program for ethics and leadership. Peter worked for 25 years as a broadcaster with the ABC. Throughout his career, Peter has combined journalism with public policy research, particularly on topics related to migration. His book, *Not Quite Australian: How Temporary Migration is Changing the Nation*, will be published in August 2016. He is also the author of *Borderline* (2002), an award-winning analysis of Australia's approach to refugees and asylum seekers.

Benjamin Powell is the director of the Free Market Institute and a professor of economics in the Jerry S Rawls College of Business Administration at Texas Tech University. He is the North American Editor of the *Review of Austrian Economics*, past President of the Association of Private Enterprise Education, and a senior fellow with the Independent Institute. He earned his BS in economics and finance from the University of Massachusetts at Lowell, and his MA and PhD in economics from George Mason University. Prior to joining Texas Tech University, he taught economics at Suffolk University and San Jose State University. He is the author of *Out of Poverty: Sweatshops in the Global Economy* (2014), editor of *The Economics of Immigration: Market-Based Approaches, Social Science, and Public Policy* (2015), *Making Poor Nations Rich: Entrepreneurship and the Process of Development* (2008) and co-editor (with Randall G Holcombe) of *Housing America: Building Out of a Crisis* (2009). He is the author of more than 50 scholarly articles and policy studies.

Sudrishti Reich is a senior lecturer in the Migration Law Program of ANU College of Law, The Australian National University. She has a long-standing interest and expertise in migration law, and practised as a registered migration agent and solicitor in the field since 1997. From 1997 to 2002, Sudrishti was the principal solicitor of the specialist community legal centre Immigration Advice and Rights Centre in Sydney. She is author of two editions of the immigration law practitioners' bible: *The Immigration Kit*. Since leaving legal practice, Sudrishti has focused on teaching and developing courses in Australian migration law, and pursuing research interests in migration law and professional identity of migration agents. She teaches and develops courses within the Graduate Certificate in Australian Migration Law, and the Master of Laws in Migration Law. Sudrishti is General Editor of *Immigration Review*, published by LexisNexis.

Shanthi Robertson is a Senior Research Fellow at the Institute for Culture and Society at Western Sydney University. Her research centres on migration, mobilities, citizenship, and urban space, particularly the social, cultural, and political consequences of contemporary modes of migration governance in the Asia-Pacific. She is the recipient of a 2015–18 Australia Research Council Discovery Early Career Researcher Award for a project on temporality, mobility, and Asian temporary migrants to Australia. Her work has been published in various international journals, including *Ethnic and Racial Studies, Journal of Ethnic and Migration Studies, Journal of Urban and Regional Research, Citizenship Studies, Ethnicities, City and Community, Journal of Intercultural Studies and Population*, and *Space and Place*. Her first book, *Transnational Student-Migrants and the State: The Education Migration-Nexus* (2013), was awarded the 2014 Raewyn Connell Prize for the best first book by an author in Australian sociology.

Sanmati Verma is a senior lawyer and registered migration agent with extensive experience in the immigration law field, having worked with the Civil Justice Section of Victoria Legal Aid and Clothier Anderson Immigration Lawyers — a specialist immigration law firm based in Carlton. Sanmati specialises in complex immigration matters, including protection applications involving identity and exclusion issues and character-related matters, including those involving the Australian Security and Intelligence Organisation. Sanmati also has regular conduct of a broad range of immigration matters at the primary, merits, and judicial review stages, and has conducted litigation across all courts of federal jurisdiction, including the High Court of Australia. Sanmati has published extensively in online and print media on topics related to global immigration. Sanmati has held voluntary positions with the Australian Muslim Civil Rights Advocacy Network, Footscray Legal Centre, and Western Suburbs Legal Service, and was the founder of the International Student Legal Advice Clinic, which opened in Melbourne in 2009.

www.ingramcontent.com/pod-product-compliance
Lightning Source LLC
Chambersburg PA
CBHW040149270326
41927CB00029B/3424